TRE

MW01248889

Far-Out Grandparents!

…More than 700 ideas for Grandparents
(and all other relatives and friends) who
want to maintain a helpful, warm
and loving relationship
with the children
they treasure…

Carolyn Brooks

Gainesville, Florida
352 333 8958
cbrooks126@aol.com

Xulon
PRESS

Far-Out Grandparents!
by Carolyn Brooks

Printed in the United States of America

Library of Congress Control Number: 2003103080
ISBN 1-591605-16-4

Xulon Press
10640 Main Street
Suite 204
Fairfax, VA 22030
(703) 934-4411
XulonPress.com

To order additional copies, call 1-866-909-BOOK (2665).

To Betty —

No wonder it's
called "great" and
"grand" parenting — it
certainly is!

For Dad —

Carolyn Brink

DEDICATION

This book is dedicated to my family...

To my husband, Hugh...
my patient champion throughout this project!

To my parents, Katherine and Allen Bowling...
my exemplary grandparenting pattern!

To my daughter Katie ...
my spirited booster every day!

To my son David and his wife Sally...
my precious connection between generations!

and

To my grandchildren, Emily and Zachary ...
my delightful inspirations for this book!

ENDORSEMENTS

"This is a recipe book for grandparents near or far. The ideas for bringing and keeping the little ones close are so creative, fun, and helpful. What a <u>grand</u> idea!"

- **Jane Powell, Author and Star of stage, film, television, and radio**.

"This could be characterized as a 'how to' book. How to do the right things as a grandparent and not interfere with the parenting. This book has wonderful ideas for being a loving, teaching, and guiding grandparent. In my case, I was raised by loving grandparents, and I treasure the wonderful security they brought to my life which lasts until this day. Joy and I have a new grandbaby, and it's a new journey. This book will help."

- **Ralph Emery, Author and Star of television, stage, and radio**.

"Wish you could erase the miles between you and your grandchildren? Carolyn Brooks' new book helps you do just that. Far-Out Grandparents is a book packed full of great ideas for keeping a fun and close relationship with your grandkids to matter how far away they are. I highly recommend it!

- **Martha Bolton, Author of more than 40 Christian books, and Bob Hope Staff Writer for 15 years.**

"Far-Out Grandparents! Is a blockbuster book with endless great ideas for keeping your grandchildren close to your heart. It's creative and carefully written. At points it's philosophical ('Give the gift of self-confidence: praise them') and at the same time practical. A good read for any grandparent. I only wish its author Carolyn Brooks had been MY grandmother."

- **James L. Terhune, Professor of Journalism and Communications, University of Florida.**

CONTENTS

PREFACE

Hello there! I'm Carolyn Brooks. I've been married to Hugh Brooks for about 567 years. Well, certainly for most of my life. We have two children, David and Katie. David and his wife Sally have two children...our grandchildren...Emily, age 18, and Zachary, age 16.

Emily and Zachary were born at West Point when David, a career soldier, was teaching there. Since they were born, their family has lived in Hawaii, Germany, Kansas, Georgia, Washington State, and Pennsylvania.

Each time they moved we tried to get the Army to assign them to our house. But we haven't been persuasive enough...

So we're always living away from our grandchildren. We're always "far out" grandparents.

In spite of the distances, however, we try to maintain an "everyone is living in the same area" type of relationship. Even though separated, we are growing up with our grandchildren. It isn't easy to do this, but it's well worth the necessary effort.

I've been saying "our" and "we" in these first few paragraphs, because my husband's love for our grandchildren and his participation in the task of keeping us all growing together is essentially a part of everything you'll read here.

This book is an attempt to relate our "stay-together" pilgrimage by listing some of the activities we have generated in that quest, and adding to those the ideas we have gathered from other sources. It is written primarily for grandparents who are away from their grandchildren. But it is also for all grandparents...the "far-out" kind and the "everyone at home" kind...as they work at the process of attempting to maintain a helpful, warm, and loving role in the lives of their grandchildren.

It is impossible to use the word "grand" without implying a value judgment, and this book is written with the view that purposeful interaction between grandparents and grandchildren will make life better for both. The introduction is an expression of this possibility as I believe it. The book itself lists activities and resources that grandparents may use to turn that possibility into reality.

There are religious activities in the listings, because many activities that my husband and I judge to be character building are derived from our religious experiences and commitments.

No work of this kind could cover every conceivable activity and every family circumstance. And no grandparent can suggest all the innovations that other grandparents might devise from a single activity. I have chosen, therefore, to list the activities and the resources with as little editorial comment as possible...to give you a "starting place."

It would be impossible for a grandmother to leave a page like this without giving one word of advice. I must. Read this book with a highlighter in hand! You'll run across dozens, perhaps hundreds of "eureka" ideas! Mark them now. Use them later!

I have written this book with the hope that some of the

things mentioned would help you and your grandchildren know each other better, help each other grow, and love each other more.

Carolyn Brooks

INTRODUCTION

In the 1960's, the hippie and flower child generation repeatedly used a phrase that ingrained itself in our culture…"Far out, Man." They meant "cool," "neato," and "hep." Those 60's young people are now grandparents. And many of them, along with other loving grandparents, give an entirely new, and now, poignant meaning to "far out." They live "far out" from their grandchildren.

Our nation is mobile. America's roads are traveled every day by thousands of trucks and other motorized vehicles, and a large percentage of the trucks are moving vans being used to transport household furniture as Americans change homes and locations.

Many of the people involved in those residence moves stay within the areas where they have previously lived, but more than 75 per cent move to different counties, different states, and even different countries. Usually they leave behind some members of their family. More often than not, this separates grandparents and grandchildren. Statistics show that more than 50 per cent of American grandparents and grandchildren now live more than 500 miles from each other.

"Far out, man."

The phrase would be humorous here if it were not so painfully descriptive of a situation that diminishes one of the most meaningful relationships of human experience and makes much more difficult the unique opportunity that grandparents and grandchildren have to assist each other in growing and learning.

Child psychiatrist Arthur Kornhaber says of this relationship, "The attachment between grandparent and grandchild is second in emotional power and influence only to the relationship between parents and children. But there is an important psychological difference between the two. The normal tensions between parent and child simply do not exist between grandparent and grandchild."

"The normal tensions simply do not exist..." What an opportunity for loving grandparents! Grandchildren do want to be close to them! In a national survey, children 9 to 16 stated that what they want most from grandparents is love, care, encouragement, fun, support, and interest. They expressed an overwhelming desire for grandparents to be involved in the "growing up" process!

The writings of leading child psychologists and family counselors describe the vital roles open to grandparents in the lives of their grandchildren. They indicate that grandparents can be:

- **Historians.** They can preserve the past and give grandchildren a sense of belonging to a greater, more inclusive ongoing scheme of life.
- **Moralists.** They can protect from pitfalls and give grandchildren direction for their lives by sharing tried and true morals grounded in faith and religion.
- **Educators.** They can promote learning and assist grandchildren in using the communication skills essential in a complex world.

- **Mentors.** They can prepare grandchildren for the future by teaching responsibility for time, money, and talent, as well as by advocating conservation in the world around them.
- **Supporters.** They can labor in love to provide the praise that weaves character and happiness into the fabric of a rich, full life.

Far Out!

But can "far out" grandparents enjoy those roles? Anthropologist Margaret Mead said, "Three hundred years have now developed a style of family in which there is little expectation of much closeness in residence or care between grandparents and grandchildren. Thus the problems of building lasting relationships between first and third generations and being able to share advice and contribute significantly to their lives are compounded."

Compounded indeed! But not impossible! Never! Concerned, loving grandparents find ways to be everything they can be for their grandchildren...historians, moralists, educators, mentors, and supporters...even if they live hundreds of miles apart!

This book offers activities that can help keep grandparents and grandchildren "together," regardless of the distance between them.

These are IDEAS! Most of them can be done from a distance, although many are written for those times when grandparents and grandchildren are together. If you like some of the "together" activities, but simply must remain "far out," then tell your own children what you'd like to do...they'll be delighted to help you adapt those "together" activities to "far out" use.

Selecting and initiating activities requires dedication, creativity, and adaptability, but what effort could produce more meaningful results? At the "grandparenting" age, many loving family members have time, freedom, an abundance of experience, and at least some small amount of discretionary money available. To use these with and for their grandchildren will be to enrich the present and insure the future. These grandparents will be:

Grandpreservers! Grandprotectors! Grandpromoters! Grandpreparers! And Grandpraisers!

James Lee Ellenwood, in his book *One Generation After Another*, uses a youngster's prayer that sums up the need and the possibilities for grandparents and the grandchildren they love:

"Dear God, please help the old folks understand the young folks. May there be between them a lasting bond of friendship and affection and a strong partnership and mutual respect. As they live together may each learn from the other in true humility. And, if it is not asking too much, may the endless rendezvous of one generation with another be a lot of fun for both. Amen."

Far out...

CHAPTER ONE

THE GRANDPROCEDURE

*"Don't let distance get in the way. Be willing
to use modern technology...to keep in touch"*
Lillian Carson

In her delightful and helpful book, *The Essential
Grandparent: A Guide to Making a Difference*, Lillian
Carson lists DOs and DON'Ts for grandparenting. The
quote used above is one of the DON'Ts. When describing
modern technology, Ms. Carson mentions pagers, e-mail,
and faxes. She might well have included four other techno-
logical wonders that are essential components of modern
communication...telephones, letters, tapes, and computers.

Grandparents who will not let distance get in the way
have all these methods of communication available
to them. Telephones and letters are familiar and convenient, of course, and if grandparents prefer to use only
these, the activities listed in this chapter are worth consideration. Newer methods of communication, however, offer

opportunity for innovation and variety that both grandparents and grandchildren may find enjoyable and productive.

Your grandchildren <u>will</u> be using these new communication wonders. Dr. Arthur Kornhaber urges you to join them... "Let your grandchildren take you by the hand and lead you into the future. Computers, fax modems, rules about playing soccer, new research in math and science— whatever seems intimidating and beyond your grasp are but made comprehensible and fun by the gentlest and most eager of teachers, your grandchildren."

Communication is the essential element of all growing human relationships. Without meaningful communication you may be a grandparent, but you cannot be a *Grandpreserver*, a *Grandprotector*, a *Grandpromoter*, a *Grandpraiser* , nor a *Grandpreparer*! **Stay in touch with your grandchildren!**

Stay In Touch With Your Grandchildren... Use The Mail

Stay In Touch With Your Grandchildren... Use The Telephone

Stay In Touch With Your Grandchildren... Use The Fax Machine

Stay In Touch With Your Grandchildren... Use The Computer

Stay In Touch With Your Grandchildren... Use Audio And Video Tapes

Stay In Touch With Your Grandchildren... Use Personal Visits

Stay In Touch With Your Grandchildren... Use The Mail

Try these things...

- Establish a routine for letters and packages to your grandchildren. Purchase and stamp twelve business-sized envelopes or nine-by-twelve manila envelopes at the beginning of the year. Stamp these with your name and address. Give them to your grandchildren. Ask them to drop papers, pictures or other sharing items into one of these envelopes each month and mail it to you.
- Address and stamp envelopes to send to your grandchildren while addressing and stamping envelopes for them to send to you. Use plain envelopes or envelopes you create from colorful magazine pages. Regularly send the grandchildren photos, items or information about your life. Visual reminders establish a vital presence for them.
- Purchase, address, stamp, and store a variety of cards with monthly themes and special messages for use throughout the year. At the beginning of each month, write and send notes of encouragement, love, praise, or general information.
- Send picture postcards from every place you visit on your travels. Select them with care for possible use in a school project.
- Turn snapshots into "personal travelogue" postcards with messages. Address them and write notes on the backside. Note: According to mail regulations these must be no smaller than 3 fi x 5 inches and no larger than 4 fi x 5 inches. Use a 23-cent stamp.

- Re-use greeting card fronts as postcards. Tear off and discard the back panels. Postal requirements also apply to these.
- Invent and use a catch phrase or personalized signature to end all your written communications. Make this a fun touch.
- Write letters in Morse code. Look up the meanings of the dots and dashes in any good encyclopedia under "International Morse Code". Tell your grandchildren how they can find the key to translate your messages.
- Send secret messages. Using wax paper over a sheet of white paper, draw or write with a pencil to press the wax line into the paper underneath. Label the correct side (the side with the wax impressions). Send instructions to apply a thin coat of paint over the labeled side of the paper and the message will appear.
- Create a nonsense picture through the mail. Begin by making a few lines or shapes on a blank piece of paper. Mail it to your grandchildren. Ask what they see in the drawing. Tell them to add to your drawing and send it back to you. Next, you tell them what you see in the drawing. Mark it again and send it back. The last one to add to the drawing saves it until your next visit together. It becomes a conversation piece.
- Make a photograph collage placemat of you and a grandchild. Mail it so you can have a "presence" at every meal.
- Surprise your grandchildren with a life-size poster. Lie on a large piece of paper and have someone draw around your body. Cut out the body form. Place it in a large manila envelope and mail. Instruct your grandchildren to "clothe" and

decorate using crayons, markers, or colored pencils.

- Use a shirt cardboard to make a hanging "good-night sign." Paste pictures on the sign of you and your grandchildren that were taken in your bed, in a rocking chair, in a porch swing, a hammock, or in another favorite sleeping place. Laminate the cardboard. Punch two holes in it and add string or ribbon for hanging. Include a note explaining that you will be there every night to say goodnight.

- Glue an enlarged photo of yourself on a shirt card-board. Cut it into puzzle shapes. Send the pieces in an envelope. Tell your grandchildren that someone who loves them will appear when they put the pieces together.

- Trace the paw or foot of a family pet. Send it and ask the grandchildren if this is a critter they know.

- Send a package of forget-me-not, morning glory, and primrose flower seeds for an ongoing, shared, morning and evening flower-growing project.

- Send small envelopes filled with things your grandchildren can identify by smell—mint leaves, cinnamon, cloves, orange or lemon peels, flower petals, pine needles, and baby powder. Use a separate envelope for each aroma. Number these. When you talk, ask your grandchildren to identify each and to share the information with you.

- Send instructions for simple science projects for little ones. Get these in your public library.

- Send small envelopes filled with things your grandchildren can identify by touch through the envelope--a key, a feather, a small stone, a leaf, a pencil, a button, a coin, and a safety pin.

- Mail some dried beans, lima beans, or corn kernels with instructions to soak the seeds overnight in water and then put them on a moistened paper towel. The seeds will soon start to sprout. Tell the grandchildren to plant them in a pot or in the garden.

- Place one-fourth cup of alfalfa seeds in a small plastic bag. Mail with instructions to soak seeds overnight in water, rinse and drain, and keep them out of the sunlight for four more days. On the sixth day, place the seeds in sunlight to cause them to turn green.

- Select a picture of something familiar to your grandchildren such as the family pet or a swimming pool or slide. Cut off part of the picture of the familiar object. Mail the main part of the picture, and tell your grandchildren to draw whatever is missing. Send the other part of the picture in the next mailing.

- Create a sewing card. Draw a simple figure such as a boat, kite, kitten, duck, or house. Instead of making a solid line around the figure, make it with dots spaced a half inch apart. Thread a plastic needle with yarn and mail both in one package.

As you receive mailings from
your grandchildren, think of ways
to preserve what they send you.

Try these things...

- Laminate artwork or writing samples. If you do

not have access to a laminating machine, self-laminating pages are available at office supply stores or variety stores such as Wal-Mart or K-Mart. Office supply stores will do the laminating work for you for a small fee.

- Use these laminated treasures for place mats when your grandchildren come to visit, or frame them and hang them on your walls. Give some to your grandchildren for use in their rooms.
- Collect a supply of bargain-priced frames from garage sales, flea markets, Good Will stores, Big Lots stores, and other bargain outlets. Use these to frame artistic renderings.
- Put inexpensive precut mat boards (handmade or purchased at crafts and discount stores) over paintings or drawings. Clip the art and matting together with colorful spring clips or paper clips. Place these on plate racks for display on mantels, coffee tables, or bookcases.
- Reduce or enlarge drawings for framing by using copying machines at grocery, variety, and office supply stores. Cost is usually ten to fifty cents per page.
- Copy artwork for use as gift-wrap or stationery.
- Create a memory chest from large, sturdy boxes. (File boxes are excellent.) Decoupage these, paint them, or cover them with fabric or paper. New decoupage methods are fast and easy. Iron Wonder Under^{TM} on to fabric for covering boxes. Local arts and crafts stores will help with suggestions and supplies.
- If you are skilled in the art, handcraft chests from wood. At graduations or weddings, present your grandchildren handcarved keepsakes filled with life memories.

Stay In Touch With Your Grandchildren...
Use The Telephone

Try these things...

- Watch for special "best rate" deals in newspapers, magazines, mail advertisements, telephone billings, and correspondence from organizations such as alumni clubs, travel agents, and fraternal organizations. Remember that long distance phone rates vary from carrier to carrier and according to the time of day and day of the week. Check out Dime Line as one reasonable calling service. Call 1-800-583-6767. Or ask your present telephone service provider to give you a better rate than you have now.
- Obtain a toll free Call Box 800 Service that will allow you to trade messages with family members as you travel. Ask your telephone service provider. If you are on AT&T, call 1-800-233-0075, ext. 101, for information.
- Consider a personal 800 number to make it easier for grandchildren to call you. Ask your telephone service provider.
- Purchase a prepaid calling card for grandchildren going on vacation or to college. Average cost is $18 for 120 minutes.
- Purchase a speakerphone to share conversations with others in the room.
- Subscribe to an electronic mail system for voice messages. Ask your telephone service provider.
- Get pictures of your grandchildren talking on the phone. Place these next to your phone. Update the photos from time to time. Provide the grandchildren with similar photos of you to place by their phones.

- Begin a regular "update" call to your grandchildren. Choose a time that is convenient to everyone and touches base with as many members of the family as possible.
- Make your chats come alive with heartfelt questions and with enthusiasm for the things your grandchildren consider interesting. Pick up clues from the children or their parents.
- Speak kindly. These conversations will remain etched in memory.
- Converse in a manner that will help your grandchildren learn to speak and think more clearly. Ask open-ended questions, pay special attention to feelings, draw out your grandchildren, and show them you really are listening.
- Keep a notepad by the phone to jot down thoughts from your grandchildren's stories so that you can refer back to them. Keeping track of these details shows that you listen and that you care.

Stay In Touch With Your Grandchildren... Use The Fax Machine

Try these things...

- Use a fax machine or fax modem to instantly transmit your messages. The cost of sending a fax is the cost of a very brief long distance phone call, and in many circumstances will be less than the cost of a first class stamp. If you don't have a fax machine, send and receive faxes at an office supply store. The response can be immediate and gratifying.
- Ask your grandchildren to have someone take Polaroid pictures of special events, photocopy

them, and fax them to you ASAP.

- Enlarge a personal photo or a photo of a special and meaningful event to eight and one-half by 11 inches and fax it to your grandchildren.
- Greet the day for your grandchild with a short fax message of encouragement.
- Close the evening with a faxed goodnight wish, prayer, or thought about the day.
- Be the first to say "Happy Birthday" or "Congratulations" with a fax on the morning of that special day.
- Fax pages from coloring books for your grandchildren to color. Request that they return them to you.

Stay In Touch With Your Grandchildren... Use The Computer

Computer on-line communication allows you to keep in touch with family members at a distance quickly, consistently, and inexpensively. Consider purchasing a computer and printer. Even inexpensive computers provide e-mail, chat rooms, voice mail, access to the Internet, and fax capabilities. You <u>can</u> learn to use computers. Do it!

Stay In Touch With Your Grandchildren... Use Audio And Video Tapes

Some of life's greatest pleasures come from seeing the faces and hearing the voices of your grandchildren. If you can't often be with them in person, audio and video tapes are excellent substitutes.

Try these things...

- Pass a video tape back and forth. After filling the

tape, erase, and reuse it or place it in a video library. Be sure to carefully label it for easy retrieval.

- Videotape over instructional videos that come with new appliances and products to produce short videotaped postcards. This is an inexpensive, quick, and easy way to keep the family up-to-date and in touch.
- Entertain your grandchildren by sending videotapes of yourself doing things such as playing peek-a-boo, singing "Head and Shoulders, Knees and Toes," "Twinkle, Twinkle Little Star " or other classic children's songs.
- Sing lullabies or read stories and poetry on audio or video tape. Purchase "read aloud" books from your bookstore or borrow them from your local library. Read to tape your own favorite books, or books that were favorites of your children. Books and songs on tape can be particularly useful when neither mom nor dad is available at naptime or bedtime.
- Videotape news broadcasts on the day your grandchildren are born and on their succeeding birthdays. These tapes will become a running remembrance of the prominent personalities and historic events of your grandchildren's lifetimes.
- Videotape a "tour" of your home before your grandchildren visit.
- Prepare grandchildren for a visit by sending a videotape of the neighborhood and places they will see. Take them for a walk around the yard. Introduce them to neighbors and other people they will meet.
- Videotape parts of your environment that your grandchildren do not experience. For a grandchild who lives in Hawaii, a grandparent who lives in

snow country can videotape a snowman or snow angel. A grandparent who lives near the ocean can videotape the beach and a sand castle for a child who lives inland.

- Document the growth and development of family members and pets with a video camera.
- Turn familiar house sounds into a long distance game. Tape sounds such as the dog barking, a horn honking, and phone ringing. See how many of the sounds your grandchildren can identify.
- Record your voice to a cassette tape while you are cooking. Talk as you make a favorite recipe. Send the tape and a tasty sample in the same package.

Stay In Touch With Your Grandchildren... Use Personal Visits

When it's time to visit, the old theatrical adage "leave them wanting more" is probably a good guideline. Don't stay too long. But while you are there make your visit a special occasion. Celebrate.

Try these things when you visit your grandchildren...

- Bring presents. These don't have to be expensive, but they should be thoughtful.
- Talk about your grandchildren's activities.
- Ask questions and discuss their problems.
- Teach a skill.
- Tell funny stories.
- Plan a project to complete with your grandchildren while you are visiting.
- Decide together on projects to undertake during

the year, such as keeping journals or researching the family genealogy.

- Tell stories about Mom and Dad when they were little.
- Observe children in their school setting. Talk with them about what you saw. (Ask parents to check with teachers well in advance about spending some time in the classroom and/or having lunch at school.)
- Plan an outing or an evening at home just with your grandchildren.
- Be helpful by assisting with dishes, toy pick-ups, washing, ironing, mending and other necessary jobs.
- Bring comfy clothes for entering a child's world on the floor or on the playground.
- Become a player, fully involved in whatever your grandchildren imagine.
- Laugh, dance, and sing together.
- Touch gently.
- Read books aloud.
- Establish traditions for your visits. Say "We'll do this again on our next visit."
- Chronicle your visit in a journal.
- Take photos during your visit and write a story about them for your grandchildren.
- Leave something behind to let the memory of your visit linger. It could be cookies, vegetables in the freezer, a special cake, or a flower or shrub planted in the garden.
- Hide a treasure before you leave. When you get home, make a treasure map with clues and send it.
- Leave a note behind in the paws of a favorite stuffed animal, under a pillow, or in a shoe.

Try these things when your
grandchildren visit you...

- If possible, have one grandchild at a time.
- Create an itinerary or a photo calendar of outings and events planned for the visit.
- Plan to be as flexible and relaxed as possible during the visit.
- Be well rested.
- Clear your date book and clarify your priorities so that you can spend as much time as possible with the children.
- Prepare a welcome banner. Hang it on the door or in a window.
- Create a paper pathway of foot shapes or arrows from the front door to the children's room. Move the cut-outs around to help your grandchildren locate the way to the breakfast table or bathroom or to a hidden surprise.
- Say yes as often as possible!
- Say no when necessary.
- Honor their feelings.
- Build a whole bunch of blanket forts.
- Fly kites together.
- Walk in the rain.
- Go barefoot.
- Stay up late together.
- Let your grandchildren help with household chores.
- Make time for naps and quiet times.
- Let the grandchildren cry.
- Borrow, rent, or buy the right equipment, essentials, and toys to assure a pleasant visit.
- Ask your local furniture store for empty boxes of all sizes. These can create a constantly renewable

wonderland of houses and kitchens and trains and cars.

- Visit your local library to research games and books appropriate for the ages of your grandchildren.
- Make small picture albums from construction paper, small plastic bags, and staples.
- Make play dough from household items. Let your grandchildren help with the preparations. Here is the recipe:

    1 cup water
    1/2 tsp food coloring
    1 tsp vegetable oil
    1 cup flour
    1/2 tsp cream of tartar

    Cook over medium heat for 3 to 5 minutes, stirring until it hardens. Place on waxed paper to cool. When cool, place in baggy to knead until smooth.
- Request that parents prepare your grandchildren for visiting with your pets.
- Be sure to display the pictures, gifts, and treasures your grandchildren have sent.
- Allow grandchildren to choose a "special place" to explore during each visit. Try an attic, a closet, a sewing room, a toy chest, a drawer, a basket, or a cupboard.
- Make available a child-size chair, a desk, or a table for art projects.
- Assemble a fun-time supply of paper, crayons, stickers, tape, markers, paper punches, paper towel tubes, shoeboxes, corks, newspaper, milk cartons, egg cartons, magazines, paper bags, and envelopes.
- Plan some cooking projects.
- Ask your grandchildren's parents for advice about

the tastiest way to make sure the little ones get nutritional essentials.

- Plan some main meals ahead and freeze them.
- Keep grandchildren on a routine and on familiar foods.
- Talk early and often to your grandchildren's parents about established priorities and rules.
- Know what is going on in your area that will be of interest to your grandchildren. Browse through newspapers, and call the local children's libraries and museums for ideas.
- Establish "riding in the car" ground rules.
- Review and be prepared to teach games that will entertain children who are constrained by an automobile seat belt.
- Capture the best moments of the visit by starting a project to be updated each day. Consider a diary, a mural of each day's activities, an illustrated storybook, photos, or a videotape. Keep parents updated on the visit of the grandchildren with daily e-mail, faxes, or telephone calls.
- Slip notes into your grandchildren's socks, shirts, and books when they pack to leave. They will discover surprise messages weeks and months after their visit.
- Draw the floor plan of your house on interfacing material purchased from a local fabric store. Cut out each room and mail it to your grandchildren to reassemble as a visit reminder. Include pretend-furniture made of felt or flannel.

CHAPTER TWO

THE GRANDPRESERVERS

"Find your grandparents. Talk to them. Learn all you can from them."

Alex Haley

Alex Haley, the author of Roots, told an audience that the secret of wisdom and the foundation for worthwhile decision making lies in learning as much as possible from what has gone before us. His recommendation, quoted above, was a suggestion that almost all grandparents will appreciate and understand. Grandparents have experience, wisdom, and perception that can be invaluable to the young, and especially to those who are family...their own grandchildren.

Heritage and hope are inseparably joined. The promise of a secure, productive, and joyful future that grandparents want for their grandchildren will be immeasurably enhanced if it is built on a strong relationship both to the historical foundations of individual families and to our nation of freedom. Caring grandparents can be a dynamic link to the past for their grandchildren…a link that strengthens the chain of continuity and of hope. <u>Help your grandchildren preserve the past</u>!

Preserve Your Grandchildren's Family History
Preserve Your Grandchildren's Own Legacy
Preserve Your Grandchildren's American Heritage

Preserve Your Grandchildren's Family History

Try these things…

• Trace the family roots and write a family genealogy. Seek help with your research from:
  * Private agencies such as the National Genealogical Society in Arlington, VA., LAMP Genealogical Research (Call 1-800-838-2080), or local societies listed in the yellow pages of your phone book.
  * Computer programs such as *Roots V For Windows, Ancestral Quest and The Family Tree Maker* by Broderbund Software. These programs are available from Parsons Technology, 1700 Progress Drive, PO Box 100, Hiawatha, IA 52233-0100 or call 1-800-223-6985.
  * Books in the library such as *Searching For Your Ancestors* by Gilbert H. Doane, University of Minnesota Press, Minneapolis, MN, or How To *Climb Your Family Tree by* Elizabeth Queener, Eggman Publishing, Inc., Nashville, TN.
  * Your grandchildren. Encourage them to interview family members.
• Develop a family tree, display it on a tree design

made of fabric, on poster board, on a window shade, or by a timeline on the back of a wallpaper border.

- Collect family history in scrapbooks. Use a loose-leaf binder with a section for each family member. Include mini-biographies, photographs, and, when available, a collection of writings by that person—letters, poems, and schoolwork.

- Research the family coat of arms. Make copies of the family coat of arms for your grandchildren and ask them to tell you what they think the symbols and wording mean. Ask them to give reasons for the use of the symbols. Suggest they create a modern family coat of arms giving thought to colors, symbols, phrases, etc. Ask them to write an explanation of their own designs. Copy these and give to family members as gifts on special occasions. If you do not possess a copy of your family's coat-of-arms, research it in the 'Heraldry' section of your library or consult professional researchers.

- Preserve the old family Bible. The old family Bible may tell the story of the past in your ancestors' s Consider copying these pages and sharing them with all family members. Take special care to save the family Bible for future generations. It would be impossible to replace it.

- Transform tattered quilts or old bedspreads into delightful stuffed toys or ornaments. You don't have to construct masterworks. Even a trinket is a treasure if it is your personal creation.

- Frame pieces of antique quilts. Cut quilts into picture framing sizes large enough to show the quilt pattern. Mat and frame the pieces. Write a brief note about the history of the design and of the family member who created it. Attach the note to the back of the frame. Give to your grandchildren.

- Cut and mount pieces of an old quilt. Cut hearts, flowers, circles, or squares, mount them on boards covered with complementary fabrics, and frame them. Use cookie cutters as patterns.
- Frame doilies and other handwork. Crocheted, knitted, embroidered, or tatted pieces are priceless forms of art. Write a brief history of the person who made each piece and a description of the craft involved. Attach it to the back of the picture.
- Teach crocheting, knitting, tatting, woodcarving, or similar creative skills to your grandchildren. If you do not have these skills, and if your grandchildren show an interest, find someone who does and persuade them or pay them to perform this service for you. Your concern and persistence will benefit your grandchildren throughout their lifetimes.
- Arrange and mount memorabilia in shadow boxes, printers' trays, glass-topped coffee tables, or in picture frames. Gloves, dance cards, scarves, jewelry, letters, and pins preserve a history of their times and the people who owned them.
- Introduce your grandchildren to old-fashioned games. Teach them checkers, dominoes, shooting marbles, jumping rope, jacks, and pitching washers. Teach them to cut out paper dolls and snowflakes from accordion- folded paper.
- Suggest additional old-fashioned games for playing at family picnics or reunions. Ask your grandchildren to research rules and make preparations for activities such as horseshoes, egg tosses, sack races, cakewalks, and pie-eating contests.

- Mail an old object such as a darning egg, a razor strap, a shoe form, a buttonhook, or a tatting shuttle to your grandchildren. Ask them to identify the article and describe how it was used.
- Share an inexpensive but sentimental item from your past. Share a dance card, a compact, a key ring, a political button, a club pin, a pocketknife, a coin, or a college pompom. Write and include a paragraph or story about the object, telling what it meant to you in the past.
- Search the attic for something you owned or made when you were your grandchild's age and give it to your grandchild. Explain its meaning.
- Write an autobiography. Write about your life, even if you don't consider yourself a writer. Make the manuscript available when it is finished, or leave it in a private file to preserve your insights for your children and grandchildren.
- Begin a written family record. Information passed by word of mouth tends to become confused or forgotten. Interview family members. Share the interviewing and recording task with children and grandchildren.
- Record elderly relatives. Make an audio or video tape recording of an elderly relative telling stories of the past, reciting favorite poems, or singing cherished songs or hymns.
- Make a one-year memory calendar. Purchase or assemble notebooks with 365 pages, one page for each day of the year. Assign one notebook to each older family member. Ask grandchildren to write a different question on each page about the lives and times of these people. The recipients will write answers to one question each day. (Examples of questions: What was your favorite toy? When did

you learn to swim? Did you ever deal with a bully?) Help grandchildren think of other questions.

- Compile a family cookbook. Ask family members to contribute favorite recipes and to include anecdotes or stories relating to them. Be sure to include the recipes for your grandchildren's favorite foods.
- Preserve the songs and lullabies you sang to your children by writing them in booklets and presenting them to your grandchildren.
- Transplant cuttings from family gardens for your grandchildren. Pass along a rose bush from a great, great grandparent's garden! Your grandchildren will enjoy taking care of the plant.

Preserve Your Grandchildren's Own Legacy

Try these things...

- Piece quilts or naptime/television-viewing throws. Cut quilt pieces from grandmother's old dresses, grandfather's ties or shirts, children's outgrown clothes, baby blankets, old college team sweaters, or sweatshirts. Back the quilt with heavy flannel or a similar fabric.
- Create a newborn's hat from an old handkerchief. The baby can wear the hat home from the hospital or at the christening, then the parents can put it away and plan to use it again on a wedding day. After removing the stitches, the hat will become a handkerchief again. If the hat belonged to a girl, she carries the handkerchief with her wedding ensemble. If it belonged to a boy, he presents it to his bride.

- Start a "keepsake" chest. Use old trunks, yard sale chests, antique boxes, family cedar chests, or chests of your own construction. Fill them with special knickknacks, jewelry, handmade items, household items and other family treasures you would like to preserve for your grandchildren. Present these when they graduate from school or marry.
- Decoupage a memory box. Paint shoeboxes or filing boxes and their lids with poster paint. ModPodge™ flat, paper souvenirs such as post cards, autographs, newspaper articles, pictures, photographs, or tickets from sporting events, shows, museums, and amusement parks on the boxes. (Note: ModPodge™ is in most crafts stores.)
- Initiate a music comparison project. Discuss and compare the music of your day and the music of today. Consider music production, instruments, artists, names of songs, dances, styles, and fads associated with the times.
- Take your grandchildren to the attic, garage, basement, or storage area of your home when they come to visit. Let them explore. And prepare to answer questions!
- Save copies of newspapers, popular magazines, sheet music, albums, and "fad" information on each birthday. Gather these in a safe place until the child is grown.
- Collect a comprehensive time capsule package of memorabilia on the day your grandchild is born. Include newspapers, recordings of song hits, a birth announcement, a list of guests who came to visit the newborn, coins of the birth year, stamps, videotapes of newscasts, family photos, and

a personal letter from you about the joy of the birth. Keep these in a safe place until time to open the capsule.

- Write or record on audio or video tape all the family happenings on the day your grandchild is born. Be sure to include humorous anecdotes from and about relatives and other people involved in the circumstances of the day.

- Ask each family member to mold an object from clay for the newborn. Create a mobile. Ask donors to sign and date their objects. Use a theme such as Noah's ark, nursery rhymes, toys, or circus animals.

- Give picture books of relatives and pets to newborn grandchildren. Mom and Dad can use the books at bedtime to acquaint your grandchildren with the family.

- Ask family members to trace hands on fabric squares for a quilt. Use fabric markers or embroidery around the hands. Give the quilt to the new grandchild.

- Design items that remind your grandchildren of special times in their lives. A blizzard in a jar recreates a winter storm. Layering colored sands in a jar reproduces a seascape reminder of summers at the shore. A mural of wild animals on a window shade can remind children of a trip to the zoo. Ask participants at a birthday party to sign their names or to draw around a hand on the tablecloth using fabric markers, crayons, or pencils.

- Create memory trunks for graduating grandchildren. Decorate a trunk with bits and pieces of home, high school memories, or representative lifestyle preferences to use at college as an end table for storage in the dorm room. Stock it with

care packages, clothes, keepsakes, or memories.
• Start charm bracelets. Expand them through the years by adding charms periodically. Select charms with special meanings for your grandchildren.
• Begin a tradition of sending an annual good-luck charm at the beginning of each school year. Send small pocket-sized objects as reminder of your love.
• Make decorative stepping stones for the garden when grandchildren come to visit. Use masking tape to reinforce pizza boxes for molds. Mix Quickcrete® mortar and water in a bucket until it resembles thick frosting. Pour into molds. Let children decorate with hand or footprints, coins, glow-in-the dark adhesives, rocks, beads, buttons, small tiles, or broken pieces of china. Add grand-children's names and the dates of the stone creations. Let the stones dry in a protected area. When dry (after 24 hours), gently turn over the mold and pop out the stone. (Note: Kits that include molds and cement are available in most crafts stores for about $10.)
• Make heirlooms of hands or footprints in dough. Mix the following ingredients in a large bowl: 4 cups flour, 1 cup salt, 1 tsp. Alum (grocery or drug stores), 1-1/2 cups of water. Knead until dough is smooth. Roll out a thick circle of dough on a floured counter. Direct grandchildren to put a foot or hand in the circle, then sign and date it. Use a straw to preserve a hole in the top for hanging. Transfer the mold to an ungreased baking sheet and cook at 275° for thirty minutes. Turn it over and bake for another 1-1/2 hours until dry and hard. If desired, paint the mold and seal with clear nail polish. Leftover dough can be

refrigerated for several weeks. Add color to dough with food coloring. Use for creating many fun things.

Preserve Your Grandchildren's American Heritage

Try these things...

- Instill the principles of the Bill of Rights and the Constitution by studying together the founding principles of our nation. Obtain copies and try to put the concepts into words that your grandchildren can understand. Let your grandchildren tell you what they think the meanings are, and you share your definitions.
- List the freedoms and rights mentioned in magazines and newspapers for a month. Discuss the list with your grandchildren.
- Research historical eras together. Pick specific time frames in American history. Research and discuss information about the music, flags, uniforms, dress, customs, and heroes of those times.
- Search library files for old newspapers from the Civil War, and the World War I and II eras. Make copies of interesting articles and ask your grandchildren to compare them to today's newspapers.
- Purchase and share the book and tape, *Take Off Your Hat When the Flag Goes By*. These are introductions to the Constitution. They help children understand and appreciate the concepts of freedom and how government functions in America today. The tape has sixteen upbeat songs and informative and entertaining dialogue.

Price is about $10.95. Call BRITE MUSIC©, (801) 263-9191, for information.

- Visit significant historical places and museums. Take your grandchildren with you if possible. If you visit without them, be sure to collect materials and information to share with them.
- Create opportunities to discuss meaningful patriotic topics with your grandchildren. Suggest these topics: "What America Means To Me," or "Why Are People Willing To Die For Their Country."
- Acquaint grandchildren with the meanings of military awards, accomplishments, and ranks. Many military family members received patches, pins, medals, and ribbons. Some children become so fascinated by these artifacts that they collect them.
- Purchase and share coloring or cutout books with historical themes.
- Show your patriotism by showing respect for the American flag. Stand and salute when asked to do so at public affairs. Fly the flag on appropriate holidays. Learn proper flag etiquette. Share the history of the flag. Write for information to The National Flag Foundation, Flag Plaza, Pittsburgh, PA. 15219
- Teach grandchildren the songs of our nation's significant historical past. Look in the public library for *America The Beautiful, Stories of Patriotic Songs* by Robert Kraske.
- Discuss the words to the National Anthem. Introduce your grandchildren to verses not commonly used. Tell them the song's history and ask them to write a song for our country. A good source book is *Our National Anthem* by Stephanie St. Pierre, Millbrook Press, 1992.

- Read together historical fiction based on fact. There are many wonderful children's books of this kind available in libraries or book stores.
- Write a story about a favorite historical person with your grandchildren. Pretend the historical person visits America today. What differences are apparent between today and the time that person lived?
- Purchase and share computer software that teaches the history of our country through games. Consider *Bring U.S. History and Geography to Life, Kids Learn America*, and *The American Girl Series*. These can be purchased through *The Edutainment Catalogue*TM. Write to PO Box 21210, Boulder, CO 80308 or call 1-800-338-3844.
- Encourage the reading of biographies of great Americans.
- Pretend to be a famous, historical character. Invite your grandchildren to conduct an imaginary interview.
- Expose grandchildren to our country. Take your grandchildren to other states and cities. If you travel without them, collect free materials at welcome centers in each state. Send them maps and markers so they can trace your trip routes.
- Suggest that your grandchildren write "request for information" letters to Departments of Tourism in each state and to Chambers of Commerce in cities.
- Help grandchildren recognize states by their shapes. Purchase and share coloring books, cutout books, puzzles, maps, magnets, and sticker books that teach these skills.
- Purchase and share a large outline map of the United States. Challenge your grandchildren to

see how many news items and pictures they can uncover about each state in a month. Tell them to place the items on the map over the appropriate states.

- Challenge your grandchildren to become authorities on one state. Make a notebook of all the information that can be collected about that state. This can be a year-long project.
- Initiate a sports travelogue. Select a favorite professional sports team with your grandchildren. Using an outline map of the United States, locate the hometown of the team. Tell them to follow the team's travels in the newspaper. Record what states, mountains, and rivers the team will pass through as it travels to game cities in other states. Determine the numbers of miles the team will travel.
- Purchase and share materials specifically designed to teach the geography of our country. Consider the abundance of excellent, inexpensive materials in grocery stores, drug stores, book stores, and variety stores everywhere.
- Plan visits to national parks. Obtain information from the National Park Service via the Internet (www.nps.gov/index.html) or by writing a letter to: National Park Service, 1849 C Street NW, Washington, DC 20240. Phone 1-202-208-6955.
- Take your grandchildren to visit our nation's Capitol and the historical monuments located there.
- Take your grandchildren to visit individual state capitals and museums.
- Acquaint your grandchildren with almanacs where they can research statistical information and interesting facts about each state.

- Initiate a "state of the month" project. Select one state and encourage your grandchildren to learn as much as possible about it. Send them thought-provoking statements to consider.
- Purchase and share with your grandchildren computer software aimed at teaching the geography of our country. Consider *Travelrama, USA*, and *Tour The US With Maps and Games*. These and others can be purchased at computer software stores and many book stores such as Books A Million.
- Introduce your grandchildren to the lifelong hobby of stamp collecting. The Post Office offers free information about stamp collecting and has different stamp series collectibles available. A series highlighting American history and important events during the 20th century was released recently. There is a set of stamps for each decade, 1900 through 1990.
- Start coin collections for your grandchildren. Develop themes such as animals, ships, flowers, and historical emblems. Visit hobby shops for a few basics such as coin guides, plastic storage sleeves and magnifying glasses.

CHAPTER THREE

THE GRANDPROTECTORS

"Since we've traveled further down that treacherous trail than they (grandchildren) have, it's our obligation to point out the pitfalls. Grandparents can provide a link to a secure formula of faith and common sense that can help young people stay on course and accomplish their mission."

Jack Gulledge

There is no question about what a loving grandparent would do if a grandchild happened to be in danger of being hit by a car, of drowning, of falling from a precipitous height, or of any life-threatening situation. The grandparent would intervene in any way possible to protect the child. Strange, then, that grandparents are so often reluctant to warn grandchildren of dangers that may destroy their characters and their emotional well-being and may take away their joy in living.

Jack Gulledge has offered good advice to these grandparents. It is their obligation to point out the pitfalls of life and help develop the values or virtues that will carry their grandchildren through traumatic challenges that are part of the human experience.

Values and virtues are the standards that shape who we are, how we live, and how we treat other people. In an era when traditional values and virtues are often absent from school curricula, are influenced by an entertainment industry that concerns itself primarily with the financial bottom line, and are heard too rarely even in church, it is imperative that someone teach values and virtues to our children. And there is no better someone than a grandparent!

Grandparents today are of a generation that still understands crucial virtues...trust, caring, citizenship, fairness, responsibility, respect, honesty, forgiveness, courage, happiness, gratitude, cleanliness, work, self-esteem, dependability, love, and faith. Teaching those values to grandchildren may be the most significant contribution grandparents can make to their happiness. Do it! <u>Protect your grandchildren from pitfalls...teach them values!</u>

Inspire Your Grandchildren With Faith
Inspire Your Grandchildren With Hope
Inspire Your Grandchildren With Love

Inspire Your Grandchildren With Faith

Try these things...

- Provide your grandchildren with basic age-group tools for religious study. Be sure they have—and know how to use—a Bible, a Bible concordance, a Bible topical concordance, a Bible dictionary, and a Bible commentary.
- Encourage your grandchildren to learn to use their

Bibles. Set an example for them to emulate.

- Purchase and share coloring books with Bible themes.
- Request unused or outdated literature from your church. Send religious games and activity suggestions from these books and periodicals to your grandchildren.
- Suggest weekly or monthly verses for grandchildren to commit to memory. At the end of the year give rewards for each quoted verse.
- Talk about specific Bible verses and stories. Challenge grandchildren to locate them in their Bible.
- Select Bible passages for grandchildren to memorize that are about using talents, time, and money.
- Choose Bible passages for your grandchildren to memorize that pertain to caring for God's creation.
- Pick favorite, well-known passages from your Bible and ask your grandchildren to paraphrase them.
- Encourage grandchildren to join church organizations that prepare them to understand the Bible.
- Send your grandchildren booklets that suggest daily Bible reading programs with comments about the readings. Most religious centers make these available, or you can purchase them at religious bookstores.
- Purchase or create and share yearly calendars that list daily Bible readings. Suggest the passages be read at mealtime or bedtime.
- Challenge older grandchildren to read through the entire Bible in a year's time.
- Quote your favorite Bible passage to your grandchildren. Ask them to select a favorite passage, to commit it to memory, and to quote it to you.

- Purchase and share Bible study software for your grandchildren's computers. (Example: *Daniel In The Lions' Den* by Broderbund for ages 3 - 6. Children learn the protective power of faith on their interactive journey through this story. Call Parsons Technology at 1-800-223-6985.)
- Purchase and share Bible games and activities designed for computers.
- Ask your grandchildren to send you a Bible challenge. (Example: How many times is money mentioned in the Bible?)
- Cut interesting pictures from old calendars and magazines. Mount them on construction paper or cardboard. Send them to your grandchildren and tell them to use a concordance to locate a Bible passage or passages that complement each picture.
- Purchase and share activity books from Christian bookstores that teach the use a concordance.
- Supply your grandchildren with lists of characters whose stories are in the Bible. Tell them that their concordances will help them locate these stories. On your next visit, ask them to retell some of the stories.
- Ask grandchildren to find all the names given to Jesus by others.
- Select a special story such as that of Jonah. Draw and cut out whales on which you write interesting questions about the story. Have your grandchildren find the answers and quote Bible references.
- Ask grandchildren to prepare a quiz for you so you can use your concordance.
- Ask grandchildren to make a list of all the different animals named in your Bible.
- Suggest that grandchildren use a Bible dictionary to look up the meanings of the names of Jesus.

- Encourage grandchildren to explore their feelings and read what the Bible says about them. Prepare a list of key words about feelings. Use words such as anger, sadness, fright, love, and happiness. Bible dictionaries will give meanings and references.
- Ask grandchildren to prepare a list of words for you to explore in your Bible dictionary.
- Recommend that grandchildren check to see if their own names or the names of their friends are in the Bible, and, if they are, to determine the Bible definitions.
- Explain to your grandchildren that a commentary interprets words, verses, phrases, and books. Tell them that these interpretations are the opinions of numerous people about Bible meanings.
- Suggest verses or brief Bible passages and ask your grandchildren to comment on the meanings. Then ask them to compare their interpretations with opinions in the Bible commentary.
- Purchase or create and share work sheets that allow your grandchildren to become familiar with the Bible. Ask questions such as these:
  * What is the purpose of the Bible?
  * How many pages are in it?
  * Name the sections of the Bible.
  * How many different books are in the Bible?
  * Name all the books or sections beginning with the letter A.
  * Name all the books or sections beginning with the letter L.
  * Is there a book that has a woman's name? A man's name?
  * What is the first verse in the Bible?
  * What is the last verse in the Bible?

* What is the first book in the Bible? The tenth book? The last?
* Is there a book of songs?
* Is there a book of poetry?
* Are there prophets?
* What are the names of the prophets?
* Are there books or special sections of history?
* Are there books or special sections of law?
* Are there books or special sections that are actually letters?

• Create or make use of games or songs that will enable your grandchildren to learn the names of the books or special sections of the Bible.

• Create games that will use the Bible as a resource. Example: Develop an elementary acrostic and tell the grandchildren to circle the words "our God is love."

> **o u r t w**
> **a n g p q**
> **j i s o r n**
> **z x d f g**
> **d e v o l**

• Purchase or create and share crossword puzzles with Bible questions and answers.

• Purchase and share figurines that represent the great heroes and stories of the Bible (an example, a Nativity set). Give one of these on baby's first birthday or one each Christmas. Add pieces each year. Consider a process that would begin with the first character or characters mentioned in the Christmas story and add the remaining figures periodically. If you are together on Christmas, set aside time to read the Christmas story from the Bible. Discuss the piece of the nativity given that year. Be sure to prepare written presentations bout those pieces for your grandchildren to keep. Add various pieces of scenery when the collection of main characters is complete.

- Maintain activities related to the figurines throughout the year. Purchase or create and share books, games, pictures, quizzes, and activities relating to the theme.
- Make a nativity collection a one-year project. Send one piece each month starting in January. Include ideas about Bible study concerning the meaning of the pieces.
- Purchase and share a collection of one kind of Christmas symbol such as angels or stars. Send one of these each month or each year at Christmas.
- Encourage grandchildren to pray.
- Tell your grandchildren about answers to your prayers.
- Tell grandchildren to keep a diary of prayer requests and answered prayers
- Mount photos of friends and family in a book next to spaces for written prayer requests. Entitle these books "Prayer Portraits."
- Tell your grandchildren about your religious experiences. Do it in person or in writing.
- Write letters of joy and support when your grandchildren publicly acknowledge their faith.
- Teach your grandchildren the standard songs of your faith and let them teach you today's new songs.
- Encourage grandchildren to pray aloud at mealtime.
- Teach your grandchildren to remember others in

their prayers. Show them how to make prayer lists for each night for a week.

- Read Bible stories aloud at bedtime when grandchildren come to visit.
- Keep Bible story coloring books and activities on hand to use when grandchildren visit.

Inspire Your Grandchildren With Hope

Try these things...

- Purchase and share helpful videos produced by famous people. (Example: Tom Selleck's *Kids For Character.*)
- Purchase and share music with character building words that grandchildren can memorize. Music is stored in our long-term memory. When we learn something through music, we tend to remember it longer.
- Be an example. Tell them of your hope.
- Purchase and share *Brite* Music products for your grandchildren. *Brite* Music is one of the nation's leaders in music education. The *Standin' Tall* series offers books and audio cassette sets with such titles as "*Obedience*," "*Honesty*," "*Forgiveness*," "*Work*," "*Courage*," "*Happiness*," "*Gratitude*," "*Love*," "*Service*," "*Cleanliness*," "*Self-Esteem*," and "*Dependability*." Cost is reasonable. The company offers videos entitled "*Play It Smart, Stay Safe From Drugs*," "*Personal Safety*," and "*Protect Their Minds*" and continues to add award-winning material that children love. Call (801) 263 - 9191 and ask about a representative in your area.
- Stay on the alert for additional audio tapes, books, CDs, videos, movies, and television programs that

reinforce positive-living concepts. Preview these, and recommend your selections to your grandchildren. Start with the public library!

- Purchase and share the book entitled *God's Little Instruction Book For Kids* published by Honor Books, Inc., Tulsa, OK.
- Purchase and share *The Book of Virtues*. This book provides every family member access to some of the greatest literary works of all time. It champions a reliable moral reference point for our culture, our history, and our traditions. The 831-page volume is available at book stores and discount membership warehouses such as Sam's Club for about $20.00.
- Purchase or create and share bracelets, pins, and necklaces with sayings that are reminders the great virtues. Guiding Light® offers a bracelet called The Humanity Bracelet. Call 1-800-659-7667.
- Make a list of ten virtues with your grandchildren. Select one virtue each week to examine and discuss.
- Keep a running journal of those times you recognize outstanding character qualities in your grandchildren.
- Collect clever sayings and use them on sweatshirts, tee shirts, drawings, needlework, patches, or on hats. Examples:
  * What you sow is what you grow.
  * Beauty shines through in the good that you do.
  * Obey now, play later. Disobey now, pay later.
  * Make the one who's left out your special friend. Do for other people what you want them to do for you.
  * Whatever you say, whatever you do, bounces

off others and comes back to you!
* The "Be" Attitudes—Be kind to others, and you will find kindness coming back to you.
* The thoughts that you think are up to you. What you think is what you do.
* Increase the peace.
* It is good to do good.
* Helping hands make happy hearts.
* It's not what you get but what you give that determines the worth of the life you live.

Inspire Your Grandchildren With Love

Use some of your time, some of your energy, and some of your compassion to help people in need, then teach your grandchildren to do the same thing. Try to get involved in one or more of the following activities yourself, and talk to your grandchildren about working with you or about getting involved in some of the others. Always share your experiences and your compassion with such enthusiasm that your grandchildren will want to be involved in service to others.

Try these things...

• Encourage your grandchildren to make a list of organizations in their communities that need volunteer help. The Community Chest may have a beginning list for their consideration.
• Encourage your grandchildren to volunteer. Suggest that they enlist more people to become involved in volunteer activities.
• Help keep public parks, lake areas, rivers, and highways clear of litter.
• Assist the sick, the elderly, or new mothers with light housekeeping and yard work.

- Make attractive tray favors or cards for hospital or nursing homes.
- Learn to assist handicapped adults or children as they develop new skills such as skiing, horseback riding, bowling.
- Assist with construction and renovation projects for low-income families.
- Start a small telephone check with elderly or sick people.
- Volunteer to feed a pet, water flowers and yard, collect mail and check on the house for neighbors going on vacation.
- Call someone who does not drive or own a car and arrange to take them to the grocery store, to doctor's appointments, or on necessary errands.
- Collect food and clothing for someone whose home burned or was destroyed in a natural disaster.
- Consider raising a guide dog for the blind. Look for local information on this project in the yellow pages of your phone book under *Blind Services and Facilities*.
- Share a pet with someone at a nursing home or with an elderly neighbor.
- Be a big sister or brother to a disadvantaged youth.
- Be a special friend to a new student at school or in the neighborhood.
- Read stories at children's centers to children with busy, working parents.
- Walk a dog or help with pet care for an invalid or elderly person.
- Tutor younger children, especially those whose parents work.
- Collect fabrics and make "ugly quilts" for the homeless. For free directions send a self-addressed envelop to:

My Brother's Keeper Quilt Group
Strawberry Hill Farm
RD 1, Box 18824
Hop Bottom, PA 18824
Or phone: 1-570-289-4335

- Fix a dessert, a salad, or a meal for a family with sickness, a family with a new baby, or a family in bereavement.
- Make a May Day basket of flowers and hang it on the front door of a neighbor as a surprise gesture of goodwill.
- Leave a special treat in the mail box for the letter carrier.
- Say "thank you" in a special way to public servants such as police officers, garbage collectors, teachers, etc.
- Invite someone who is far from home to share a meal or a special holiday in your home.
- Invite an orphan for a vacation at your home.
- Sponsor an orphan.
- Offer your services to help build playgrounds, churches, or teen centers.
- Volunteer to read newspapers, novels, magazines, or children's books over the radio for the blind.
- Volunteer at an animal shelter.
- Volunteer to serve meals at a homeless shelter.
- Raise money for a meaningful charity.
- Collect food for a food bank. Help sort, stack, and store it.
- Provide an "extra pair of helping hands" at a day-care facility.
- Assist at a thrift shop by sorting, storing, and straightening shelves or by clerking.
- Answer phones or do clerical work or data processing for hospices, nursing homes, and

non-profit organizations.
- Help pack informational kits for hospitals, nursing homes, and non-profit organizations.
- Volunteer for ground care and/or building maintenance at non-profit organizations.
- Escort patients at hospitals or nursing homes.
- Deliver magazines, newspapers, and additional reading materials to patients.
- Assist nurses with non-medical duties.
- Deliver meal trays at hospitals or nursing homes.
- Provide clerical assistance for labs and clinics.
- Assist patients with personal tasks such as writing letters and phone calls.
- Show movies at nursing homes or extended-care institutions.
- Serve refreshments to patients.
- Assist with games for patients at nursing homes or extended-care institutions.
- Teach arts and crafts projects at nursing homes.
- Provide entertainment for nursing homes or veterans hospitals.
- Help patients participate in daily activities such as hobbies, crafts or special programs.
- Read books, stories, papers, and magazines to patients.
- Take patients for walks outside or to sunrooms.
- Work in gift shops at hospitals.
- Push wheelchair patients to special events.
- Take pictures of happy moments that extended-term care patients can view later when times are not so happy.
- Visit patients whose families are far away.
- Enlist more volunteers.
- Make "trauma dolls" for children entering the hospital. These are soft, cloth dolls made with

fabric and batting. Pattern books in fabric stores have directions for cloth toys.

- Volunteer to rock newborn babies in hospitals.
- Collect baby clothing and accessories for new mothers who are having financial problems.
- Contribute good, used items for resale to organizations such as Good Will or the Salvation Army.
- Tutor children who are confined at home or in a hospital for a long time.
- Prepare and deliver a basket of snacks and juice to family members waiting at the hospital.
- Donate your frequent-flyer miles to distant family members who cannot afford to fly if there is a lengthy or severe illness and those members need to be at the bedside.
- Give a needy family gift certificates from restaurants that deliver meals.
- Send balloon bouquets, funny cards, posters, toys, or humorous books to hospital patients to boost spirits.
- Offer to give family members a break from hospital room vigils.
- Loan a portable computer to a patient or to family members at the hospital.
- Take toys, puzzles, games, picture books, coloring books, and age-appropriate computer games to children in the hospital.
- Volunteer to care for a sick person's pets.
- Assist out of town families in finding a place to stay that is near the hospital.
- Donate blood to replenish the general supply.

CHAPTER FOUR

THE
GRANDPROMOTERS

*"Education is not preparation for life.
Education is life itself."*

John Dewey

From 1884 to the time of his death in 1952, the work of
John Dewey was significant in re-structuring the use of
the basic components of education...listening, speaking,
reading, and writing. His emphasis on learning through
varied activities rather than formal curricula was largely
responsible for the monumental change in teaching
methods that began in the United States early in the 20th
century, when emphasis shifted from the institution to the
student.

The advocates of so-called progressive education have
often-misinterpreted Dewey's theories, but his philosophy
has become ingrained in both the formal classroom setting
and the informal education methods of family, friends, and
associates. His contention that "education is life itself" is a
pedagogical call to arms for every member of society who

would have any part in re-structuring life as we now know it for the benefit of lives yet to be lived.

Marian Wright Edelman brought the educational philosophies of the life classroom and the centrality of the student directly into the everyday American family mainstream. She wrote that "Parents (and by implication, Grandparents) have become so convinced that educators know what is best for children that they forget that they themselves are the experts."

Parents…and grandparents…are the experts! What a wonderful concept!

As informal education "experts," grandparents are twice blessed. They have knowledge to share, and they have opportunity to make use of varied activities that will promote education proficiency by their grandchildren. Innovative grandparents can ignite a learning fire that will warm all of education for their grandchildren and help weave the mosaic that defines the very fabric of the persons these grandchildren will make of themselves. <u>Promote education in the lives of your grandchildren!</u>

Help Your Grandchildren Learn Vocabulary
Help Your Grandchildren Learn To Speak
Help Your Grandchildren Learn To Listen
Help Your Grandchildren Learn To Write
Help Your Grandchildren Learn To Read

Help Your Grandchildren Learn Vocabulary

Try these things:

• Purchase and share a thesaurus. These invaluable resource books are available for most age and skill levels. They are available at most grocery, variety, discount, or book stores.

- Encourage the use of a thesaurus.
  * Write some sentences for grandchildren to re-word using the thesaurus.
  * Write a "pretend" letter to a celebrity or cartoon character. Ask your grandchildren to re-write it with the help of the thesaurus.
  * Cut a paragraph from a newspaper, magazine, or book and ask your grandchildren to re-write it with the help of the thesaurus.
  * Listen carefully as your grandchildren talk. Notice and write down common words that they tend to use frequently. Encourage them to replace those with new, more descriptive words from their thesaurus.
  * Make a list of some common English words. Ask your grandchildren to search out antonyms and synonyms of these words in the thesaurus.
- Tear out monthly *Reader's Digest* columns entitled "It Pays To Enrich Your Word Power." Mount each column (with answers on the back) attractively. Send these as games to your grandchildren.
- Compile several "It Pays To Enrich Your Word Power" columns from *Reader's Digest* into attractive workbooks. Leave these in the car to use as the family travels and commutes.
- Create and share word power pages of your own. Develop specific topics such as flying, weather, scuba diving, and sports. Enclose these power page words in correspondences with your grandchildren.
- Encourage grandchildren to listen to and read the weather reports each day. Suggest they keep a list of weather words and learn their definitions.

- Collect action words from sports headlines with your grandchildren. Make a poster using these words.
- Challenge your grandchildren to make a list of all the phrases that sports editors use to say one team defeated another team.
- Create and share word games that will introduce grandchildren to professional vocabularies. Use words unique to the legal, engineering, health/medical, and religious professions.
- Place easy adverbs on cards in a hat. Let grandchildren draw and act them out, one word at a time, and have someone try to guess the word.
- Select a page from a magazine. Ask your grandchildren to circle with crayons all the nouns in red, the verbs in blue, the pronouns in green, the adjectives in orange, and the adverbs in purple.
- Assemble booklets of word puzzles, crossword puzzles, unscramble word puzzles, and hidden word puzzles from newspapers and magazines for your grandchildren to complete.
- Challenge your grandchildren to locate specific words in newspaper and magazine articles and advertisements.
- Cut black-and-white pictures from newspapers or magazines. Ask your grandchildren to write descriptions of the pictures using as many color words as possible.
- Tear pages from magazines or columns from newspapers. Invite grandchildren to underline words of emotion with colored pencils. (Example: Happy words with green, angry words with red, energetic words with yellow, and sad words with blue.)
- Use *Mad Libs* for a variety of vocabulary-building activities. *Mad Libs* is a name for tablets of letters

and stories designed for children to fill in blanks and complete the text. They are available at bookstores, toy stores, drug stores, and grocery stores.

- Teach grandchildren how to use the dictionary, the thesaurus, and new computer programs to dissect and analyze words.
- Purchase and share computer word games. (Example: *Word Games and Crossword Puzzles* by Infomath. The cost is $14.95 or two for $24.95 in the *Edutainment Catalog*™. 1-800-338-3844.)
- Search in your local library for books that teach basic etymology, including word components, numerical prefixes, and borrowed and invented words. (Examples: *10 Minute Guide To Building Your Vocabulary* by Ellen Liechtenstein, Alpha Books, New York, NY, 1997; and *How To Build A Better Vocabulary* by Elizabeth Ryan, Troll Assoc., 1992.)

Help Your Grandchildren Learn To Speak

Try these things...

- Recommend that your grandchildren work extensively with audio tape. Suggest that they use a tape recorder to:
  * Relate incidents from experiences at school.
  * Read or tell stories.
  * Interview someone.
- Recommend that your grandchildren narrate home videos.
- Correspond with your grandchildren by audio tape. Include other relatives, friends, or pen pals in this project.
- Recommend that your grandchildren prepare

readings, poetry selections or monologues to present at family gatherings or special events.

• Advise your grandchildren to enter competitions that require speaking skills.

• Suggest that your grandchildren pretend to be disc jockeys and that they prepare an audio tape of fifteen minutes of music and talk for a radio show.

• Ask your grandchildren to audio tape "live" presentations of their favorite comic strips.

• Suggest that your grandchildren act out their favorite comic strips for audiences of younger siblings or neighborhood friends.

• Initiate talk shows for family gatherings or parties. Ask grandchildren to be hosts.

• Encourage grandchildren to run for class offices at school.

• Recommend that grandchildren audition for school or church activities that require speaking skills, such as making announcements over the intercom system and introducing guest speakers.

• Suggest that your grandchildren participate in thespian activities.

• Play games with your grandchildren that require choosing words. (Example: I'm going on a trip. I need to pack _____. Start with the letter A, have the second person add a B item, then add a C item, and work through the alphabet. Take turns adding each item. Have each person repeat the entire list of items before adding a new one.)

• Play games with your grandchildren that encourage talking.

　* Present an idea and see how many story variations you can invent. (Somewhere a phone is ringing--who hears it? Who is calling? What happens next?)

* Bring characters to life. Choose a name from history. Ask grandchildren to describe the character—looks, clothing, and attitude.
* Make a list of common, everyday actions (jumping, winking, tapping feet). Talk about the many different ways people use these actions.

• Encourage your grandchildren to act out amusing family stories. (Example: Little Roberta climbing on the table and sitting, bare bottomed, on the freshly iced birthday cake.)

• Create and share simple puppets from socks, fingertips of old cotton gloves, popsicle sticks, tongue depressors, wooden spoons, or cardboard. Write a puppet show together. Plan for grandchildren to act it out at a family gathering.

• Introduce a familiar or imagined story. At one point, stop and pass the story to your grandchildren to continue. Pass it back and forth until completed.

• Read the classified ads of the newspapers to locate job opportunities for people with speaking talents. Bring these to the attention of your grandchildren.

• Read the book, *Wild Words! How To Train Them To Tell Stories* by Sandy Asher, Walker and Co., New York, 1989. Pass along some of these methods to your grandchildren.

Help Your Grandchildren Learn To Listen

Try these things...

• Encourage your grandchildren to listen to a variety of music. *Bottom Line* says music may boost intelligence.

- Plan daily singalongs when your grandchildren are visiting. Sing songs with choruses that can be easily repeated and memorized.
- Play games with your grandchildren that require them to match your handclapping patterns.
- Purchase and share a recording of *Peter and The Wolf* to teach grandchildren how to listen for various instruments in the orchestra. Try different recordings to heighten their abilities to recognize other instruments.
- Hum or whistle familiar tunes to your grandchildren. Let them guess the names of the songs. Allow them to whistle tunes for you to guess.
- Listen to newscasts and weather reports. Discuss these with your grandchildren through the mail, on the computer, on the phone, or in person.
- Suggest that grandchildren listen to newscasts on television or radio and that they read a daily newspaper. Compare the coverage of the same items in their area and wherever you happen to be.
- Suggest that your grandchildren listen to news conferences held by the President and to take notes during the conference. Compare their notes with yours and with newspaper and television accounts.
- Check the classified ads of the newspapers and mark the job opportunities that need good listening skills.
- Give your grandchildren oral directions for a task that requires several steps to complete.
- Challenge grandchildren to listen for new words in television programs and conversations. Suggest they write these words in a notebook, search out the definitions, and try to incorporate them in their own conversations.

- Suggest that grandchildren listen for accents used by other people and try to identify their place of origin.
- Ask grandchildren to listen to bird calls and to try to reproduce them.
- Assist grandchildren in answering questions correctly and interestingly in telephone conversations.
- Play games with your grandchildren that require repeating rhythm patterns or word groupings. (Examples: Tap rhythms with a spoon on a pie tin, have grandchildren listen and try to repeat the rhythm; recite poems or verses with repeated verses," There was an old woman who swallowed a fly, I don't know why she swallowed a fly...")
- Use familiar finger plays or "handies" with small children. (Example: "This little piggy went to market..." or "The itsy, bitsy spider went up the water spout...")
- Read aloud stories that require grandchildren to act out the reading or to follow directions.
- Read aloud poems and stories that require sound effects. Ask your grandchildren to provide the sounds.
- Pause at key words when reading aloud to grandchildren. Let them fill in the blanks.
- Recite or read poems with refrains that grandchildren can easily memorize.
- Purchase and share the book *Listen And Help Tell The Story* by Bernice W. Carlson, Abingdon Press, Nashville, New York, 1965.
- Purchase and share books with audio cassette tapes that ask grandchildren to follow directions.
- Call attention to children's television programs that teach listening skills.

- Purchase and share the computer program entitled *Earobics®*, created by Cognitive Concepts, Inc. It costs about $60.00 but has 114 levels of play per game. The program gives extensive practice for developing listening skills. 1-800-338-3844.
- Go on listening walks during one of your visitations. At some time during the walk, request that the grandchildren close their eyes and tell you what they hear.

Help Your Grandchildren Learn To Write

Try these things...

- Revive the practice of letter writing. Encourage grandchildren to write:
  * Personal letters, including: friendship, family, and pen-pals notes, thank-you notes, invitations, congratulatory notes; get-well cards, and birthday wishes.
  * General letters: to tourism departments of states and cities, to Chambers of Commerce, to tourist attractions such as Disney World, for free hobby and career materials advertised on backs of cereal boxes, on toys, or on television, and to governmental offices for school project materials about personal interests.
- Obtain the Catalogue of Catalogues from: SHOP AT HOME, SOUTH HOLLY STREET, BOX 221050, DENVER, CO 80222-9050. Then, from its pages, stock up on other catalogues like these:
  1001Things You Can Get Free
  The Sampler
  Free Stuff from Uncle Sam

Free Things For Kids
Free Stuff For Sports Fans
- Write coded messages and ask grandchildren to reply in the same code. Try these code forms:
  * Rebus--a puzzle consisting of pictures of objects, signs, and letters in combinations that suggest words or phrases.
    (a picture of a foot) + (a picture of a ball)
    foot + ball = football
  * Cryptogram--secret writing based on a key or set of predetermined rules of symbols. A=Z, B=Y, C=X, D=W. etc. Symbols can be any agreed upon code. Write the message in code. If you use the above set of symbols, (continuing through the rest of the alphabet according to the set pattern), decipher this coded message. TLLW NLIMRMT (GOOD MORNING!)
  * Hidden Word Puzzle--hidden message is among a grouping of letters. Find the words "I love you."

    I E R L T V
    S P Y O U I
    V M N V L H
    P S D E F W

- Send recipes for making invisible inks and ask your grandchildren to write you a letter using one of the inks. Make "heat sensitive inks" from common household items—work with nonfat milk, lemon, orange, apple, onion, or grapefruit juices directly. OR write with1 tsp. of either cola, vinegar, sugar, honey, salt, washing soda, bicarbonate of soda, or Epsom salt in a glass of water.

The writing will appear when held over a light bulb, an iron or an electric hot plate. Caution grandchildren about letting the paper catch fire. Don't work with an open flame.

- Make messages with cookie dough using letter cookie cutters. Request grandchildren to do the same for you.
- Stamp messages with edible printing stamps. Slice off the end of a carrot or potato. Carve a raised and reverse letter on the flat surface. Use food coloring for ink. Teach your grandchildren how to make these stamps.
- Purchase and share sponge letters for stamping messages. These are lightweight and easy to mail. Buy sets for your grandchildren to send replies.
- Ask grandchildren to write letters to advice columnists. You do the same. Trade letters and write answers.
- Become a journal writer and let your grandchildren know. Ask them to keep journals.
- Purchase or create and share attractive books with blank pages as gifts for grandchildren and encourage them to start daily journals of thoughts about special events, humorous happenings, sports events, meetings with important people, extracurricular activities, and pet antics.
- Make an agreement with your grandchildren that each of you will keep a journal for a year. Exchange journals at the end of the year.
- Ask grandchildren to keep a diary of highlights of their daily lives for two weeks. For that same period of time you clip the horoscope columns from newspapers. Compare the predictions with the events recorded in the diary.
- Help your grandchildren remember one outstanding

event in their lives. Invite them to write about this event as a newspaper article. Include a headline, and the 5Ws (who, what, where, when, and why).

- Begin a "grandparent" journal. Record humorous incidents, cute sayings, and wise observations about your grandchildren. Read these selections at family gatherings or use them to liven up an answering machine message.
- Begin one journal on the birth date of a grandchild. Enter thoughts about that child daily. Continue it until he or she leaves home. Present it as a special gift.
- Initiate "patchwork" stories through the mail. Begin a story and ask grandchildren to add to it. Continue passing the story between you until it is complete. Bind it, laminate pages, or put them in plastic sleeves. Read it as a bedtime story when they come to visit.
- Make grandchildren the heroes or heroines of "patchwork" stories.
- Compose stories and leave blanks to be filled in by grandchildren. Leave room on pages for children's illustrations. When they have returned the stories to you, follow up with sequels.
- Purchase and share books that require readers to supply endings. You and your grandchildren read the books. Each person writes an ending to the story. Compare the endings with each other and with the authors.
- Purchase and share computer programs that allow grandchildren to write and direct their own endings to stories. (Example: *The American Girl Collection*®, Collector's Tin Edition. Order by phone: 1-800-338-3844; by fax 1-800-226-1942; or by web: www.edutainco.com.)

- Collect copies of grandchildren's writings. Make them into booklets and display them in a prominent place on your bookshelf.
- Choose a personal trait or characteristic. Make up a character that has this trait. Give the character a name and ask your grandchildren to write a story about this person.
- Make a list of common, everyday feelings. Ask your grandchildren to write actions people use to demonstrate these feelings.
- Clip unusual, interesting, or funny pictures from magazines and newspapers. Send these to the grandchildren, but omit titles or comments. Ask your grandchildren to write their own titles or comments. Send them the actual titles at a later date.
- Encourage grandchildren to help spice up a family photo album. Write dialogue or captions to accompany the pictures. Or cut printed words, slogans and headlines from magazines and newspapers and paste under or around the photos.
- Write about your most embarrassing, happiest, funniest, or strangest moments and send these notes to your grandchildren. Ask them to do the same for you.
- Make "Favorite" lists with headings such as "My Favorite Song." Make these about magazines, cars, flowers, books, sports figures, games, movies, toys, colors, numbers, outfits, candies, birds, trees, Bible verses, and ice cream. Prepare the headings carefully. Send lists to your grandchildren and ask them to fill in the blanks. Exchange lists.
- Prepare "Getting To Know You Lists" for your grandchildren. Try these:

* List 1
How tall are you?
Do you like pizza ice cream? Why or why not?
What is your favorite subject in school?
What time do you go to bed on school days? On weekends?
What time do you get up in the morning?

* List 2
If you had a million dollars, what would you do with it?
Name five things you would like to have for Christmas.
What is the scariest thing you can imagine?
What is your favorite TV show?
What is your favorite color of hair?

* List 3
Name three things you collect.
Would you like to travel in outer space?
What is your best Halloween costume?
What are two things you would like to do to help someone?
What is your favorite game?

* List 4
If you could become an animal, which one would it be?
Name four careers you might like to have as an adult.
Name three careers you would never want to have.
Do you have any freckles? How many, and where are they?
Name the video games you own.

* List 5
What is your favorite candy? Dessert?
Vegetable? Meat? Fruit? Drink?
What is your favorite state? City?
What is the funniest thing that ever happened to
you?
If you could have any pet in the world, what
would it be?
What do you like best about your room at
home?

- Experiment with writing poetry. Challenge your
grandchildren to join you. Try these simple
forms:
  * Name Starters. Write a name (your grand-
    child's) along the left margin of a paper, one
    letter per line. These letters become the first
    letters of the first words on each line of the
    poem. Start a poem by filling in a letter with a
    line for the poem. Pass it to the grandchildren
    for additional lines. Trade back and forth
    until the poem is complete.

> Come play with me
> Around the tree.
> Reaching and climbing
> Over the limbs and through the
> Leaves, twigs, and branches.
> You and I find
> Nests left behind.

  * Limericks. Limericks are five-line poems. The
    first, second, and fifth lines rhyme and contain
    three accented syllables. Lines three and four
    rhyme and contain two accented syllables.

A bugler named Dougal MacDougal
Found ingenious ways to be frugal.
He learned how to sneeze
In various keys,
Thus saving the price of a bugle.

By Ogden Nash
(*Potato Chips and a Slice of Moon*, Scholastic Books)

* Puns. Puns (a play on words) are fun.

"I work as a baker,
Said Dusty Joe,
Since I'm a cake maker
And knead the dough."

By Ennis Rees
(*Pun Fun*, Scholastic Books)

* Diamante. A Diamante (Dee-ah-mahn-tay) is
a diamond shaped, seven line poem that goes
from one idea to its opposite.

Day
Bright, Cheerful
Shining, Warming, Blazing
Daybreak, Sun, Shadows, Sunset
Cooling, Darkening, Nearing
Mysterious, Dark
Night

by Michael Mager

* Haiku. Haiku (Hi-koo) is a short Japanese
poem expressing a brief, vivid thought or

observation on nature. It is usually seventeen syllables in three unrhymed lines (5 - 7 - 5).

Limbs leap to the sky
Leaves listening in the sun.
A forest --beautiful.

by Kevin Maas
(*Potato Chips and A Slice of Moon*, Scholastic Books)

* Cinquain. A Cinquain (Sin-kwain) is an unrhymed poem of five lines. Line one has two syllables, line two has four syllables, line three has six syllables, line four has eight syllables, and line five has two syllables.

Baseball
Running, sliding
The batter smacks the ball
It's soaring over the fence, gone!
Home Run!

By Theresa LaBlanc
(*Potato Chips and a Slice of Moon*, Scholastic Books)

• Encourage grandchildren to write rhymes for jumping rope.
• Encourage grandchildren to write cheers for school teams.
• Save games that have missing pieces. Ask grandchildren to create new games with the remaining pieces and to write new directions, goals, and rules.
• Encourage grandchildren to create new games. They will need to design boards and playing

pieces and will need to write rules, goals, and directions.

- Share newspaper and magazine articles on writing opportunities. *Crayola* recently offered young authors ages five to 12 a chance to submit stories to a contest and win a computer. A small article appeared in the local newspaper giving an 800 number to call and an Internet address to request rules and regulations for entering the contest.
- Mail comic strips to your grandchildren with the speaking "balloons" deleted. Challenge them to fill in the conversation.
- Mail familiar nursery rhymes to your grandchildren. Ask them to write a headline for each.
- Ask your grandchildren to write directions to their houses for you to use when you visit.
- Propose that your grandchildren write tour guides for their communities. Suggest that they include parks, places of historical interest, schools, colleges, and tourist attractions.
- Suggest that grandchildren start neighborhood newspapers.

Help Your Grandchildren Learn To Read

Try these things...

- Provide plenty of reading materials for grandchildren at their homes and in your home.
- Give book club memberships to your grandchildren. Librarians and teachers can make suggestions.
- Shop at used bookstores. Swap books and build credits for your grandchildren to use.
- Encourage your grandchildren to organize

book-trading networks in their neighborhoods.

• Suggest that your grandchildren set up lending libraries in their neighborhoods during the summer months. They can use their own outgrown collections of books, ask friends for books, or purchase books at yard sales.

• Obtain subscriptions to children's magazines for the grandchildren. Some excellent magazines are:

Jack and Jill, Turtle, Children's Playmate, Child Life, Children's Digest, Humpty Dumpty, and U*S* Kids (Ages 4-12), Children's Better Health Institute, Waterway Blvd, PO Box 567, Indianapolis, IN 46206-0567.

Boys' Quests (Ages 6-12) and *Hopscotch* (Girls 6-12), PO Box 227, Bluffton, OH 45817 – 0227.

Chickadee and *OWL* (Ages 3-9), 255 Great Arrow Avenue, Buffalo, NY 14207-3082.

Cricket, Spider, Ladybug, and *Babybug* (Ages 6 months to 8 years), PO Box 300, Peru, IL 61354.

The Friend (Christian Values), 23rd Floor, 50 East North Temple, Salt Lake City, UT 84150.

Highlights For Children (Ages 6-12), 803 Church Street, Honesdale, PA 18431.

Ranger Rick and Your Big Back Yard (Ages 3-9), The National Wildlife Federation, 8925 Leesburg Pike, Vienna, VA 22184.

Shoofly (Ages 4 - 7), PO Box 1237, Carriboro, NC 27510.

Touch (Ages 10 - 14), PO Box 7259, Grand Rapids, MI 49510.

Sesame Street (Preschool), PO Box 52000, Boulder, CO 80321-2000.

Nickelodeon (Ages 6 - 10), PO Box 11243, Des Moines, IA 50350.

Crayola Kids (Ages 4-10), Customer Service, PO Box 400425, Des Moines, IA 50340-0425.

Sports Illustrated For Kids (Ages 7-12), Time, Inc. Magazine Company, PO Box 830609, Birmingham, AL 35283-0609.

American Girl (Ages 9-12), Pleasant Company Publications, 8400 Fairway Place, PO Box 60986, Middleton, WI 53562-0986.

• Encourage your grandchildren to obtain and use public library cards.
• Refer to an invaluable resource, *Magazines for Kids and Teens*. It's published by Educational Press Association of America. You'll find it in your public library.
• Enlist your public librarian's help for motivational ideas if you have a grandchild who is a reluctant reader.
• Purchase and share books of trivia and fact books such as almanacs for reluctant readers. *World Almanac* has a kids' version. It includes fun facts, puzzles, games, and resources. ($8.95, World Almanac Books).
• Review and recommend television shows that nourish good reading habits. One program is "Reading Rainbow" on the Public Broadcasting System (PBS).
• Introduce kids to serial books. If they already read them, contribute to their collection on a regular basis. Consider these:

(Ages 0-8) <u>Dr.</u> *Seuss Books* by Dr. Seuss and *The Berenstain Bears* by Stan and Jan Berenstain, published by Random House.

(Ages 6-12) *Indian In The Cupboard* by Lynne Reid

Banks, published by Avon Books; *Boxcar Children* by Gertrude Warner, published by Albert Whitman and Co.; *Goosebumps* by R. L. Stine, and *Baby Sitter Club* by Ann Martin, both published by Scholastic; *Hardy Boys* by Franklin Dixon and *Nancy Drew* by Carolyn Keene, both published by Pocket Books; *Little House On the Prairie* by Laura Ingalls Wilder, published by Harper and Row; and *Animorphs* by Katherine Applegate, published by Scholastic.

(Ages 12-14) *Sweet Valley High* by Francine Pascal, published by Bantam Books.

- Assist your grandchildren in starting hobbies. Most hobbies require reading.
- Collect baseball cards or other theme cards for your grandchildren.
- Purchase and share models that require reading and following instructions for building.
- Play board games through the mail. Establish an on-going tournament with Gramps.
- Collect information in welcome centers at state borders and share it with your grandchildren for use with school projects.
- Search for free materials on topics of interest to your grandchildren. Refer to government agencies in the blue pages of the phone book. Encourage your grandchildren to do the same thing.
- Start "interest themes of the month." Choose a topic together. Collect as many different materials as possible on that theme. Exchange information and discuss the discoveries.
- Enhance your grandchildren's language arts education by using newspapers for a variety of activities. *The Courier Journal/Louisville Times*, Louisville, Kentucky, offers activity cards for use

with the newspaper. These activities are for children from elementary through high school ages. Each card presents problems or tasks for children to solve by using the newspaper.

- Select a person who is often in the news. Challenge your grandchildren to read about, look for pictures about, and watch this person on television for two weeks, then to write a character sketch of that individual.
- Post what you consider to be the most important daily news on a calendar for one month. Ask your grandchildren to do the same. Compare calendars.
- Play this mental exercise game with your grandchildren: Tell them to scan the front page of the newspaper for ten seconds. Use a stopwatch for timing. After ten seconds, turn the page over and write down as many topics as they can remember.
- Start a scrapbook of teenage newspaper columns for your adolescent grandchildren.
- Suggest that your grandchildren become "filler finders." Fillers are very small articles used by newspapers to fill up blank space left on a page. When grandchildren have collected fillers for two weeks, they will have an odd assortment of information to share.
- Cut a "how to" article from a magazine or newspaper. Mix up the steps. Challenge your grandchildren to put them in order.
- Share the Sunday newspaper supplement that has a children's page.
- Purchase and share "Read A Mat." These are placemats that educate. They are available at WalMart, Kmart, and kitchen supply stores.
- Consider buying each grandchild one book each month.

- Purchase books, comics, and magazines at garage sales and flea markets for the grandchildren.
- Purchase and share computer software that encourages reading. (Example: Reading Galaxy by Broderbund for ages 8 - 12. This is a reading game show that has 1,500 questions and hilarious dialogue. It is available from Parsons Technology, 1700 Progress Drive, PO Box 100, Hiawatha, IA 52233-0100. Phone 1-800-223-6985.)
- Read aloud to your grandchildren when you are visiting. Act out the stories. Ham up the acting.
- Read comic books and comic pages from newspapers aloud to your grandchildren.
- Purchase and share easy reading comic books for your grandchildren.
- Purchase and share reading games for your grandchildren.
- Plan a "Teddy Bear Picnic" when your grandchildren come to visit. Take along favorite teddy bears and teddy bear books.
- Purchase and share books-on-tape packages that include both a tape and a book. Your grandchildren can follow in the book as they listen to the tape.
- Select appropriate jokes from joke books for grandchildren to memorize and recite or to read at family gatherings.
- Send books of ghost stories for grandchildren to take to camp.
- Give bookstore gift certificates to grandchildren for birthdays and special holidays.
- Purchase and share books that identify with your grandchildren's lives.
- Purchase and share computer programs that provide a foundation for pre-readers and beginning readers. (Examples: *Curious George Readers*

Series, Sesame Street Learning Series, and Reader Rabbit Series. Prices for such programs range from $24.95 to $34.95. The Edutainment Catalog, PO Box 21210, Boulder, CO 80308 offers these along with many other educational programs. Phone 1-800-338-3844.)

- Purchase and share computer programs for older grandchildren that allow them to explore great literature of the past. (Example: English Literature Classic Bundle. Order from The *Edutainment Catalog.* Phone 1-800-338-3844.)
- Purchase and share phonics games to reinforce reading skills. *Phonics Game* for ages 6 to adult, offers 18 hours of videos and card games for playing alone or with up to six participants. Cost is $199.00. *Jr. Phonics,* for ages 3 through 6, costs $159.00. Call 1-800-965-READ.
- Mail riddles to your grandchildren. Send riddles in one envelope marked #1. A day later, send answers in an envelope marked #2.
- Purchase or create and share "blank books" for "creative" recipes. Ask grandchildren on the phone what they would put in recipes for oatmeal or chocolate cookies or pizza. Make a recipe book with the "real" ingredients on one page and the children's imaginative ingredients on the other. Let children illustrate the cookbook.
- Make alphabet books by cutting magazine pictures of objects that begin with each letter of the alphabet. Paste pictures on pages and laminate.
- Purchase or create storybooks made of fabrics.
- Purchase or create fabric books with page items that can be manipulated. Use zippers, buttons, and buttonholes, shoe laces and eyelets, safety pins and Velcro pieces.

- Make a book using grandchildren's names when they are learning to write their names. Each page is one short sentence. Grandmother loves (child's name)... Grandfather loves (child's name)... Mother loves... Daddy loves... Sister loves... Brother loves... Each time the grandchild's name is written, use a different kind of lettering from various materials such as sandpaper, yarn, fabric, pipe cleaners, and wire.
- Read books and use information from guides that offer advice on creating avid readers. Examples:

  Parents Who Love Reading, Kids Who Don't, by Mary Leonhardt

  Raising A Reader, by Paul Kropp

  Books To Grow, by Bob Keeshan (TV's Captain Kangaroo)

  Children's Books of the Year, published by The Child Study Children's Book Committee at Bank Street College. This resource provides numerous book selections for infants through 14-year-olds, tips for parents, and other special features. For more information call 212-875-4540.

CHAPTER FIVE

THE GRANDPRAISERS

"Snowflakes and fingerprints, you'll always find
Each one is different, one of a kind.
And just like a snowflake, this, too is true
No one else is exactly like you."

Author Unknown

Each person on this earth is unique, different from all others. Each has hopes, dreams, ambitions, desires, and goals that are particular and personal. Each has a singular life!

In spite of that diversity, however, all people have some needs in common...physical needs such as air and water and food, social needs such as companionship and sharing, and emotional needs such as love, understanding, and praise.

Praise? Yes. Praise. Absolutely! All people need to be reminded that they are special, and when the reminder comes with an imaginative style, the impact can last a lifetime. How important, then, is the practice of loving grandparents praising their grandchildren? Important enough that life-long positive self-image, contentment, and confidence may result.

Praise is the outward expression of love. It is one more means by which grandparents can regularly and consistently affect and nurture their grandchildren. It is inexpensive, it does not need to be taught, and it is absolutely and without question one of the happiest and most beneficial activities ever maintained in any human relationship. <u>Give your grandchildren the gift of self-confidence...praise them!</u>

Tell Your Grandchildren They Are Great
Tell Other People Your Grandchildren Are Great
Tell Your Grandchildren You Love Them By Your Actions

Tell Your Grandchildren They Are Great

Try these things...

- Write "popping" messages on pieces of paper to your grandchildren. Fold and tuck them inside deflated balloons. Mail the balloons. Tell your grandchildren to blow up and pop the balloons to read messages.
- Write messages to your grandchildren with markers on inflated balloons. Deflate and mail them. Tell your grandchildren to blow up the balloons to read the messages.
- Bake fortune cookies and place compliments inside. Mail these and suggest that the parents present them to your grandchildren on special occasions. Write messages such as: "You did a wonderful thing," "I like your style," or "Congratulations on a job well done." Messages can also be placed in wrapped candies such as Hershey Kisses and Hugs.

- Enlarge photos of your grandchildren on a copy machine and glue them to the front of Wheaties™ Cereal boxes. Send the boxes as congratulations to grandchildren for sports accomplishments.
- Send congratulatory notes when your grandchildren accomplish something special or just need a personal boost.
- Keep on hand a supply of positive, complimentary stickers to put on envelopes and packages that you mail to your grandchildren.
- Purchase and share magnets with positive messages. Grandchildren can use the magnets on the refrigerator for displaying schoolwork, artwork or other papers.
- Purchase, or create, and share yearly calendars on which you write something positive about your grandchildren each day. Look at calendars in gift or card shops and in bookstores for ideas and format. Give these to your grandchildren as gifts.
- Reward your young musicians with gold records as a pat on the back for all those hours of practice. Cover an old 45 record disc with gold paint. Use a black marker to print an original record title and the child's name over the painted label portion. Cut a piece of poster board or foam core to fit a 12 x 16 frame and glue the record to it. Add a picture of the child playing the instrument or singing or dancing. Print the achievement on an index card and glue it to the side of the picture. Hang the finished product on the grandchild's wall as a reminder of a specific accomplishment.
- Take 12 photos of your grandchildren doing commendable things while they are visiting you. Make these into monthly cover pages for

calendars. Copy and make several calendars for gifts to other family members.

• Trace your grandchild's entire body with a felt marker on a piece of butcher paper or paper tablecloth during a visit. Cut out the shape with scissors. Throughout the year ask family members and friends to write encouraging words on it and sign it. Present it on a birthday or special occasion.

• Trace the silhouette of your grandchild's head on black construction paper. Place paper on the wall. While your grandchild sits in a chair sideways, cast the shadow of the child on the paper by shining a light. Draw around the outline of the shadow. Cut out and mount the black silhouette on a large piece of white paper. Get it signed with special messages by other family members.

• Draw two hands on construction paper or cardboard. Paste together at the bottom so they appear to be clapping. Send these with a note that says I or we applaud your accomplishment or award.

• Purchase or design "special day" dinner plates. Your grandchildren use the plates on special days or for special events only. Find a contemporary ceramic studio that makes this process easy. Unlike traditional studios, where you create the pottery before finishing it, the contemporary shops provide ready-made pieces. Customers simply purchase and paint them. Cost of bisques (unfinished) pieces range between $4 and $80, and some paints are included. Studio fees are about $6 per two-hour session for adults, and less than that for children.

• Single out one grandchild for a selected time period. Send letters, cards, gifts, books, or phone calls to indicate this is his/her special time. Repeat this for other grandchildren.

- Make special pillowcases for the grandchildren's bed pillows. Use fabrics with favorite cartoon characters, colors, designs, or themes. Stitch two pockets, each about the size of a 3 x 5 index card, to the cases. If you do not sew, glue on pockets with washable glue such as *OK To Wash IT*™ or iron them on with *Wonder Under*™. Write positive sayings, encouraging words, or special Bible verses on index cards and place them in one of the pockets with instructions to read one each night, then transfer it to the other pocket.
- Decoupage large, unusual bottles with pictures, phrases, quotes, and words of praise cut from magazines and newspapers. Make the bottles into personalized lamps or let your grandchildren use them as vases.
- Design banners that fit grandchildren's personalities. Use blank wallpaper borders, paper tablecloths, rolls of computer paper, fabric pieces, or poster boards. Cut and paste personally written notes or pictures and headlines from newspapers and magazines.
- Make collages for each of your grandchildren that illustrate their uniqueness. Cut pictures, headlines, articles, comics, and advertisements from magazines and newspapers. Mount on poster boards and frame.
- Count and make notes of all the times you observe your grandchildren showing admirable character. (Examples: integrity, moral excellence, gratitude, and unselfishness). Send notes to your grandchildren on random occasions.
- Practice cheerfulness and enthuiasm. Let a sunny

disposition show your grandchildren that you enjoy their company.

- Write these words on carpet samples or small mats: "WHEN YOU NEED A HUG, STAND ON THIS RUG." Use permanent markers or fabric paint. Add the child's name and your name.
- Send "doughnut" arms of love. Cut two 16-inch "doughnuts" from a yard of fabric. Turn the printed sides of the now-donut-shaped fabric together, and sew them around the outside and inside edges. Cut through the doughnut, leaving two open ends. Pull the fabric through one of these ends to turn it right side out with the stitches inside, then stuff the donut with batting. Sew a felt hand onto each of the openings. Attach Velcro to the hands and send the finished product to a small child to encircle him or her with doughnut arms of love that can be clasped together with loving hands.
- Create "personalized love note" puzzles. Write secret messages on poster boards. Cut the posters into puzzle pieces. Send parts of the puzzles in two or three consecutive letters.
- Jot down thoughts about your grandchildren when you are apart. Add the date, time, place, and what you were doing. Save these notes in a special jar. Give visiting grandchildren "love soup." Put the notes in a pot and let them scoop them out with a ladle one by one.
- Send drinking straws with love notes attached. Cut 3 x 5 cards in half. Cut the halves into shapes of hearts, diamonds, circles, teddy bears, or flowers. Write messages on the shaped cards. Punch two holes in the cards, one at top and one at bottom. Insert the straws through the cards and mail your mealtime messages.

- Show your grandchildren how thankful you are for them at Thanksgiving. Send turkeys with colorful "thankful note" feathers. Cut basic turkey shapes from brown wrapping paper or felt. Cut turkey feather shapes of other colors from construction paper or felt. Write brief "thankful" notes on each feather. Instruct your grandchildren to add the feathers one at a time throughout the Thanksgiving season. As the turkeys "grow" feathers, your grandchildren will see how much you appreciate them.
- Send free virtual flowers and digital postcards on the computer as expressions of congratulations or praise. Two Internet addresses for sending bouquets and personal messages are: http://www.iflowers.com/, and http://www.virtualflowers.com/
- Keep a supply of Tootsie Pops® (candy suckers with chocolate inside) when grandchildren are visiting or mail some to their homes. When your grandchildren do something well, give them a "praise" pop.
- Donate books to public or church libraries in the name of a grandchild.
- Use a variety of ways to say "You're Great" on letters, on packages, on gifts, and during phone calls and visits. Use stickers and handwritten, computer generated, or stamped messages. Keep a list of phrases by the telephone. Examples:

For improvements in school work or behavior:

That's the way!	You're getting there!
Keep It Up!	You're learning fast!
Great Try!	You've done fine!
Looking Good!	You must have practiced!

Much better!   You're on your way!
Better than ever!   You're a sport!
Keep on trying!   You're improving everyday!
What careful work!   You're on the right track!
I knew you could do it! You've gotten the hang of it!
I've got faith in you!   You've made progress

For outstanding accomplishments:

Good thinking.   Good for you.
You've got it made!   You're doing beautifully!
Outstanding!   You've got it down pat!
Marvelous   What a great idea!
Hooray for you!   I'm impressed!
Superb work!   You did it!
You've earned a star!   You're talented!
Look at you go!   How clever!
Three cheers for you!   First Class Work!
Wonderful imagination!   Exactly right!
Nice Going!   Great Job!
How original!   How artistic!
Great Answer!   You've got what it takes!

When you want to say "thank you":

You remembered!
Thanks for helping!
Thanks a million!
Thanks for sharing!
How thoughtful!
How nice of you!

When you want to say "I love you":

You're #1!   You deserve a hug!

You're the best!   You make me smile!
You're an angel!   You brighten my life!
You're special!   You mean a lot to me!
You're a delight!   Super!
You're a pleasure to know!   Exceptional!
You're a real friend!   Fabulous!
You're the greatest!   Sensational!
You're one in a million!   Dynamite!
You're a gem!   Perfect!
You've got heart!   Wonderful!
There's nobody like you!   Terrific!
I'm proud of you!   What a smile!

Tell Other People Your Grandchildren Are Great

Try these things...

- Carry grandchildren's pictures on key chains, in lockets, on charm bracelets, or in lapel pins.
- Leave a message on your answering machine announcing to all callers that they have reached the home of Mr. and Mrs... Grandparents of ...
- Cover a computer mouse pad with pictures of grandchildren. Use self-adhesive, clear laminate paper over photographs to make a cover for a mouse pad. Be sure the surface is rough enough for the mouse to make contact. Kits are available in crafts stores.
- Make bookmarks with grandchildren's pictures. Copy pictures on copiers. Enlarge or shrink the pictures as needed. Laminate the bookmarks with self -laminating pages or let an office supply store do it for you. Give these to family and friends.
- Enlarge pictures of grandchildren, glue these to

pieces of cardboard, and cut into puzzle pieces. Make enough of these to share with your grandchildren and other family members.

• Create family gift calendars made from your grandchildren's artwork. Choose 12 pictures for monthly covers. Duplicate as many pictures as you need. Compile into calendars. Note family-member birthdays on the calendars.

• Create a flag or banner for each new grandchild and fly it to announce the birth to neighbors and friends. Give the flag to your grandchild for display on his/her birth date each year.

• Purchase or design auto bumper stickers with printed praise messages about your grandchildren.

• Purchase or design and wear grandchildren-praising sweatshirts or tee shirts. (Examples: Let Me Tell You About My Grandchildren; or Count Your Blessings…names of your grandchildren).

• Locate specialty shops that can transfer photos of your grandchildren to sweatshirts or T shirts.

• Wear jewelry that represents your grandchildren. Purchase Brat *necklaces/bracelets*™, or use charm bracelets, birthstone rings, or necklaces.

Show Your Grandchildren You Love Them By Your Actions

Try these things…

• Give your full attention to grandchildren when talking and listening to them.

• Call them love names and frequently use your own terms of endearment.

• Ask their opinions and answer their questions.

• Apologize when appropriate.

- Lighten up. Take pleasure in silliness.
- Share feelings. Don't hide your tears. Let them cry.
- Mitigate guilt. Help your grandchildren recognize their mistakes and admit your own mistakes.
- Share dreams. Show them how to believe in possibilities.
- Avoid making comparisons among your grandchildren. Honor their differences.
- Supervise with care. Respect their feelings.
- Seek to understand their wants, needs, and actions. Be patient. Protect them. Value their innocence.
- Love yourself and allow them to love themselves.
- Demonstrate compassion.
- Learn from them. Learn how to be open.
- Let go when it is time to let go. Let them come back.
- Keep them in your hearts and in your prayers. They have not been on earth very long.

CHAPTER SIX

THE GRANDPREPARERS

"Everything nailed down is coming loose."
Marc Connelly in *Green Pastures*

Marc Connelly wrote the Pulitizer Prize-winning *Green Pastures* in 1930 at the height of the Great Depression, but he might well have used that famous line in other times and in the midst of other world crises, for every generation must deal with the specter of Armageddon.

So must today's generation of grandparents. And so must the generations of our children and our grandchildren! Uncertainty and change are seemingly life's only certain and unchanging elements. Modern lifestyles constantly filter traditional morality, and once-accepted patterns of conduct and character are abandoned with astonishing indifference.

Our grandchildren are growing up in this kind of world! There will be too few voices encouraging them to choose the good and avoid the less good and the bad. The seasoned, concerned, loving voice of the grandparent should be one that does! Help your grandchildren prepare for the future...encourage them in the productive use of their money, their talents, and the natural resources that give them life.

Help Your Grandchildren Learn To Use Their Money
Help Your Grandchildren With Career Choices
Help Your Grandchildren Preserve Their Natural Resources

Help Your Grandchildren Learn To Use Their Money

Try these things...

- Be a good example
- See to it that your grandchildren get a regular, even if small, allowance income. This will allow them to make saving and spending decisions. Set a required structure for the allowance--some to spend, some to save, and some to give to worthy causes. (But be sure to discuss this with Mom and Dad!)
- Provide possibilities for earning extra money through additional work.
- Establish a matching funds program to help with expensive purchases. Provide a dollar for every dollar your grandchildren contribute toward the purchase. (Check this out with the parents first!)
- Teach grandchildren to set goals and priorities when they wish to purchase large ticketed items such as bicycles, clothing, sports equipment, and computer games.
- Encourage savings. Try this exercise. On the first day of the month drop a penny in a bank. Day two—two pennies. Day three—three pennies. By

the 31st day you will have accumulated $4.96. Continue each month for a year and save approximately $58.00. Challenge your grandchildren to do the same thing. Put your savings together at the end of the year and invest in the stock market. Watch the daily stock price changes.

- Suggest that your grandchildren read advertisements and compare prices for items they would like to buy.
- Discuss advertisements. Point out that their uses are to make a product look good and exciting. Discuss the difference between what the product or toy will actually do and what the advertisement claims it will do.
- Take your grandchildren on a comparison shopping trip.
- Charge interest on small loans to teach how expensive it is to "rent someone else's money."
- Teach your grandchildren about the dangers of impulsive buying. Use a list when shopping.
- Avoid bailing grandchildren out routinely. Make interest-bearing loans.
- Teach that there is no entitlement. To have money, one must earn it.
- Suggest ways for your grandchildren to become wage earners. Offer to be a financial backer to get a business started. Examples:
  * Window washer
  * Errand runner
  * Gift basket salesman
  * House sitter
  * Pet sitter or walker
  * Newspaper deliverer
  * Computer consultant

* Tutor
* House painter
* Car cleaner
* Baby-sitter
* Baby sitter broker (matching sitters with parents and getting a fee for the arrangement)
* Baked goods salesman (couple with a lemonade stand, soft drinks, ice cream, or candy bought in bulk from a members-only warehouse)
* Typist.
* Neighborhood newspaper publisher. Sell advertisements and classified ads to cover cost of printing.
* T-shirt designer (buy blank shirts wholesale and decorate with paints and iron-on transfers from a crafts shop)
* Daily phone check-in service and errand runner for the elderly (enlist senior citizens in your service and have them pay a small membership fee to be registered)
* Seller of sports collectibles
* Used books and comic books concessionaire. (Recycle books children own and no longer read)
* House and apartment cleaner
* Lawn care person (if there are a lot of kids who mow lawns in the neighborhood, try tending to shrubs and flowers or being responsible for watering)
* Co-owner in a business. (running a business with other kids in the neighborhood.)
• Collect and share guides and source information about business activities you can initiate with your grandchildren. These will be helpful:

* *The Lemonade Stand: A Guide To Encouraging the Entrepreneur in Your Child* (*Gateway* Publishers) by Katherine Nieman. This book teaches children what it takes to operate a business.
* *Ways To Make Money, The Shop At Home Catalogue.* Call 1-800-315-1995.
* *The 1998 Catalogue*, The National Center for Financial Education, PO Box 34070, San Diego, CA 92163-4070.

- Locate and support organizations that are advocates for entrepreneurial training for young people. Some of these are:
  * Junior Achievement
  * Distributive Educational Clubs of America
  * Future Business Leaders of America
  * Center for Teen Entrepreneurs
  * Business Kids
  * National Foundation of Teaching Entrepreneurship
  * Share your own experiences.

Help Your Grandchildren With Career Choices

Try these things...

- Express excitement about your grandchildren's dreams. When they indicate a desire to become a law enforcement officer or a ballet dancer, take them seriously. Brainstorm together for ways to reach the goal.
- Make lists of all the professions that can use the talents and interests of your grandchildren.
- List all the professions mentioned the newspaper for one week. Ask your grandchildren to do this.

Compare your lists.

- Suggest to your grandchildren that they make lists of all the people who keep their communities safe.
- Write an alphabetical list of careers with your grandchildren. See how many you can list.
- Write down, with help from your grandchildren, all the careers in your family.
- Talk with guidance counselors and career advisors about their theories of career choices. Share these with your grandchildren.
- Start a career resource file. As you and your grandchildren locate additional information, add it to the file.
- Cut out pictures of houses from magazines or newspapers. Ask your grandchildren to name all the different workers needed to complete these houses.
- Suggest that your grandchildren study the job opportunities in the classified sections of the newspaper, ascertain educational requirements, and compare the average salaries and advancement opportunities offered by each. Ask them to select five of these and write practice letters of application.
- Ask your grandchildren to practice writing resumes for you to critique.
- Assist your grandchildren in the search for career opportunities. Present these questions to them: What are my goals? How is my attitude toward work and other people? What are my special interests? What are my abilities?
- Take your grandchildren to the workplaces of friends in various careers.
- Introduce your grandchildren to successful

people in fields they are considering for career choices.

- Stay alert for newspaper and periodical materials on a variety of career choices related to your grandchildren's talents and interests.
- Order free government materials pertaining to the areas of interest of your grandchildren.
- Stay alert for television programming concerning career choices.
- Purchase and share computer programs that offer insight into possible careers. (Examples: *You Can Be A Woman Engineer* by Cascade Pass or *Real Science: Careers* [an insight to 28 science careers] by Videodiscovery. Call 1-800-338-3844.)
- Take your grandchildren to factories and businesses that offer guided tours.
- Nurture talent. If the talent is in the performing arts, encourage performance or demonstration as often as possible for any gathering. Frame and display artwork of a budding artist. Make a placard with the young artist's name.
- Attend professional performances or performances of budding professionals. Try to meet the performers and inquire about their field. Find out what preparations and studies are necessary. Seek information about pros and cons of this as a career choice.
- Assist grandchildren in looking for summer job opportunities that will give an insight to the careers they are considering.
- Plan for performance-oriented grandchildren to showcase for family reunions, clubs, church groups, and banquets.
- Instill in grandchildren the adage "Practice makes perfect."

- Encourage young people to research all the areas associated with their career choices. Examples: The young person interested in the music field can consider writing, performing, designing, business, law, and management. Children interested in drawing can pursue careers in furniture design, fabric design, or architecture.
- Visit museums with your grandchildren.
- Encourage exploring and expanding grandchildren's talents by offering materials from your day-to-day newspaper/magazine reading. (Example: Bob Weber, Jr. offers his How To Draw series for $3.00. The address is Weber/Draw, PO Box 5609, Riverton, NJ 08077.)
- Nourish "young artist" talent:
  * Set up a drawing space so children can return easily to unfinished work. Artists seldom finish a drawing in one sitting.
  * Collect objects, picture books, or photographs to inspire drawing projects. Most artists who create realistic works use reference material for information on shape and detail.
  * Allow children to copy from research materials, make creative changes, and combine ideas.
  * Let children under age 9 draw stick figures by themselves. Stick-figure drawings help them express feelings.
  * Remind children that artists never like all their work. Let them dislike something, figure out why, and make changes.
  * Encourage children not to throw out drawings too quickly. Let them retrace parts they like onto a new piece of paper.
  * Let children be uncomfortable when

experimenting with new media or a project that seems too hard. Explain that a new project is like learning to ride a bike or to roller skate.
* Take children to art exhibits and show them artwork books. Help them understand that there is no right or wrong way to draw.
* Encourage children to draw for themselves, not for approval. Teach them that there is no good and bad, just preference. Suggestions are OK, if the child makes the final choice. Have fun.

Help Your Grandchildren Preserve Their Natural Resources

(<u>Author's note</u>: The following suggestions are written first and foremost for GRANDPARENTS. Consider doing these things yourself, then teach them to your grandchildren.)

Try these things...

• Be an example. Become informed about issues and needs.
• Contact EnviroHealth, the National Institute of Environmental Health. The toll free hot line is at your service weekdays from 9:00 a.m. to 8:00 p.m. (ET). Technical specialists disseminate advice on a variety of environmental health issues and will search for additional information when requested. Fact sheets are mailed free of charge to consumers. Call 1- 800-643-4794.
• Use the Internet for resources. *Eco News on the World Wide Web: "Wired for Conservation,"* is a powerful educational tool for anyone interested in ecology. The site's address is: http://www.tnc.org

- Request materials from your state departments of environment and conservation. States offer free materials about air and water pollution control, ground water protection, recycling, conservation, and many other related topics. Addresses and phone numbers are in your phone book under State Government.
- Write letters to mayors, city council members, and county and state officials about stronger laws aimed at protecting the environment.
- Support laws in favor of recycling, stopping pollution, saving animals, and protecting the environment of wild animals.
- Write to world leaders and organizations about environmental concerns. Some addresses:

The President Of The United States
The White House
Washington, DC 20501

United Nations
United Nations Plaza
New York, NY 10017

Representative _____
House of Representatives
Washington, DC 20510

Senator _____
United States Senate
Washington, DC 20510

Vision
Smith Pleasant Street, #203
Amherst, MS 01002

- Search out grassroots organizations that are working to prevent pollution and volunteer some of your time to them. (See addresses at the end of this chapter.)
- Volunteer to help maintain public playgrounds, recreation areas, and other public places.
- Plan a litter day. Enlist others to assist you one day each month to clean up litter in a public place or a section of highway.
- Make new soil by composting. Build a compost box and stock with red worms to reduce the amount of garbage.
- Research topics that heighten awareness of environmental issues. (Example: Compare the benefits and drawbacks of various energy sources such as solar energy, fossil fuels, nuclear power, wind, natural gas, and electricity.)
- Follow the Pollution Index in your daily newspaper.
- Clip and save a collection of newspaper and magazine articles that explain how cities try to solve problems such as prevention of water pollution, sewage disposal, insect control, garbage disposal, or air pollution.
- Save energy. Become a "leak detective" by learning to read the water meter.
- Make a list of ways to conserve water. Compare your list with the local water company's suggestions.
- Help save the rain forests. Buy ice cream and candy made with rain forest fruit and nuts such as figs and cashews.
- Save trees. Use cloth napkins, metal forks, and reusable plates for picnics and parties.
- Determine the type of trees grown in your area and whether reforestation is being practiced.

- Learn how to plant and care for trees. Many agencies will give you information. Some will give you free trees for a small membership fee. Write: The National Arbor Day Foundation, Arbor Avenue, Nebraska City, NE 6810.
- Plant a tree in a grandchild's honor. Share information about it as it grows.
- Buy a live Christmas tree. After the holidays, plant the tree in your yard and give it a grandchild's name.
- Make Arbor Day a special holiday for planting trees, shrubs, and flowers.
- Send grandchildren to camp. The National Wildlife Federation offers Wildlife Camp for kids 9 - 13, Earth Tomorrow Camp for inner city youngsters, and Nature Link Camp for families. These provide extensive outdoor teaching activities to inspire children and adults to safeguard wildlife and other natural resources.
- Become a member of the National Wildlife Federation. Write: National Wildlife Federation, 1412 16th St. NW, Washington, DC 20003.
- Visit parks, wildlife centers, and nature preserves.
- Become acquainted with the endangered species list.
- Adopt a zoo animal. Many zoos offer vicarious adoption programs to augment the cost of animal care. For a monthly donation, zoos allow you to "choose" an animal, and give you fact sheets, photos, and stickers about that animal.
- Read books and watch television programs on animals, plants, birds, fish and insects.
- Recycle and encourage others to do so. Purchase things that come in recycled or recyclable packages.
- Refrain from purchasing toys and snacks packed

in styrofoam, plastic wrap or shiny printed paper. These are not recyclable.

- Make or purchase cloth tote bags to use for grocery shopping.
- Suggest that grandchildren make a collage of recycled things and share it with you.
- Subscribe to magazines such as Ranger Rick or Your Big Back Yard for your grandchildren.
- Seek out and promote television programming, films, and other multimedia that deal educationally with environmental issues. (Example: A video entitled *Groundling Marsh: Treasures Are For Sharing*, Lyrick Studios, 56 minuntes. Ages 3 - 7. Available at Toys R Us and other specialty retail stores for $12.99.)
- Collect conservation-themed coloring books, activity books, and cut-out books for your grandchildren.
- Buy toys that are durable.
- Buy beeswax crayons, water based markers, and recycled drawing paper for the young artists in the family.
- Contact the Audubon Society and obtain a catalogue for educational materials. Write: National Audubon Society, 645 Pennsylvania Ave., Washington, DC 20003.
- Take your grandchildren to visit national and state parks. Help them discover how these areas are being preserved for the future.
- Cultivate respect in your grandchildren for all living things. Try these activities:
  * Make bird feeders from half-gallon milk or orange juice cartons, Clorox or soda bottles, or by spreading pine cones with peanut butter. Hang these in places where your grandchil-

dren can observe visiting birds. When you talk or write to your grandchildren, ask what kinds of birds have made appearances.

* Suggest ideas for kitchen window gardens that allow grandchildren to see new growth. Potatoes, avocado seeds, carrot tops and the bottom halves of pineapples are usually used for these projects. Place potatoes and avocado seeds in glasses of water, rounded end down and held in place by three toothpicks. Set pineapple halves in bowls of water. Put carrot tops in shallow pans of water.
* Remove the top fourth of an empty egg shell. Paint a face on the remaining part, and fill it with potting soil and grass seed. In a very short time the face will grow green hair.
* Plant windowsill gardens of flowers, vegetables, and herbs that attract animals, bees, and butterflies.
* Send your grandchildren some old (clean) sweat socks and magnifying glasses. Indicate that the socks be put on over shoes for outside nature walks. Tell them to use the magnifying glasses to see how many different nature objects stick to the socks. They may want to plant some of the seeds collected on the socks or make a collage of the objects for you to see.

CONSERVATION RESOURCE ADDRESSES:

Backyard Life Habitat Program
16th St. NW
Washington, DC 20036

Isaac Walton League of America

Wilson Blvd. Level B
Arlington, VA 22209

Ecological Water Products
West Main Road
Middletown, RI 02840

Center of Marine Conservation
DeSales Street NW
Suite 500
Washington, DC 20036

Composting
Seattle Association
Sunnyvale Ave. N.
Seattle, WA 98103

Beeswax Crayons
Seventh Generation
Farrell Street
South Burlington, VT 05403

Earth Island Institute
Broadway, Suite 28
San Francisco, CA 94133

Association of Zoological Parks and Aquariums
Montgomery Ave., Suite 940N
Bethesda, MD 20814

Defenders of Wild Life
19 th Street NW
Washington, DC 20036

The Children's Rain Forests

PO Box 936
Lewiston, ME 04240
Global ReLeaf

American Forestry Association
PO Box 2000
Department WM
Washington, DC 20013

Green Seal, Inc.
PO Box 1694
Palo Alto, CA 94302

Kids Against Pollution
Tenakill School
High Street
Closter, NJ 07624

Save Our Streams
League of America
Wilson Blvd., Level B
Arlington, VA 22209
National Wildlife Federation
Leesburg Pike
Vienna, VA 22184

National Arbor Day Foundation
Arbor Lodge 100
Nebraska City, NE 68410

RESOURCES
FOR THIS STUDY

86 Ways To Say "You're Great," Item #KM-38, ©1995 The
    Positive Line, #79930.
*Kids and Their Money--Without Proper Guidance, The Two
    Are Soon Parted*, Neala S. Schwarzberg, New York
    Times News Service.
Ideas To Put Your Child On Path To Cash, Linda VanHoose,
    Lexington   Herald   Leader,   Lexington,   Ky.,
    April 8, 1996.
The Young Scientists, Cynthia Boman, Nashville Parent
    Magazine, Feb. 1996.
*The Lemonade Stand: A Guide To Encouraging the
    Entrepreneur In Your Child*, Katherine Nieman,
    Gateway Publishers.
Your Child in the Hospital, Nancy Keene, O'Reilly, $9.95.
Prime Time With Kids, Donna Erickson, The Tennessean,
    2/29/96.
Grand Loving, Sue Johnson and Julie Carlson, Fairview
    Press, Minneapolis, MN, 1996.
Wonderful Ways To Love a Child, a Motivational Poster by

Judy Ford, MSW Human Relations Consultant.

Computer Crafts for Kids, Margy Kuntz and Ann Kuntz, Ziff-Davis Press.

Empty Your Pockets, Start A Coin Collection, Bob Howard, The Tennessean, 4/28/96.

The Edutainment Catalog, PO Box 21210, Boulder, CO 80308.

The American Numismatic Association, 818 North Cascade Ave., Colorado Springs, CO 80903-3279. Phone 1-719-632-2646.

God's Little Instruction Book For Kids, Honor Books, Inc., Tulsa, OK.

One Generation After Another, James Lee Ellenwood, Charles Scribners Sons, NY, 1953.

Mad Libs, Roger Price and Leonard Stern, Price/Stern/Sloan Publishers, Inc., Los Angeles, CA.

NIE, Newspapers in Education, The Courier Journal/Louisville Times Activity Cards, 525 W. Broadway, Louisville, KY 40202.

How To Win Grins and Influence Little People, Clint Kelly, Honor Books, Tulsa, Oklahoma, 1996.

Songs In Action, R. Phyllis Gelineau, McGraw-Hill Book Co., 1974.

Wishes, Lies, and Dreams, Teaching Children To Write Poetry, Kenneth Koch, Vintage Books, New York.

Patriotic Songs Of America, John Hancock Mutual Life Insurance Company, Boston, MA 02117

Printed in the United States
945600003B